Dealir
Emotior

Life Coaching

This book is a comprehensive guide for life coaches on how to react and adapt when emotional problems get in the way of coaching. Windy Dryden uses rational-emotive and cognitive behaviour therapy techniques to offer advice on:

- when it is and is not appropriate to work on emotional problems
- when the coach should refer the client to someone else, such as a psychotherapist or counsellor
- how to use RECBT to help clients with their emotional problems within a life coaching context
- at what point it is sensible to begin coaching again.

Dealing with Clients' Emotional Problems in Life Coaching will be a valuable resource for all those involved in life coaching.

Windy Dryden is Professor of Psychotherapeutic Studies at Goldsmiths College, London.

Dealing with Clients' Emotional Problems in Life Coaching

A Rational-Emotive and Cognitive Behaviour Therapy (RECBT) Approach

Windy Dryden

Routledge
Taylor & Francis Group

LONDON AND NEW YORK

First published 2011
by Routledge
27 Church Lane, Hove, East Sussex BN3 2FA

Simultaneously published in the USA and Canada
by Routledge
270 Madison Avenue, New York, NY 10016

*Routledge is an imprint of the Taylor & Francis Group,
an Informa business*

© 2011 Windy Dryden

Typeset in New Century Schoolbook by
RefineCatch Limited, Bungay, Suffolk
Printed and bound in Great Britain by
TJ International Ltd, Padstow, Cornwall
Paperback cover design by Andrew Ward

This publication has been produced with paper manufactured to strict
environmental standards and with pulp derived from sustainable forests.

British Library Cataloguing in Publication Data
A catalogue record for this book is available from the British Library

Library of Congress Cataloging-in-Publication Data
Dryden, Windy
   Dealing with clients' emotional problems in life coaching :
   a rational-emotive & cognitive behaviour therapy (RECBT) approach
   / Windy Dryden.
      p. cm.
   Includes bibliographical references
      1. Personal coaching.   2. Rational emotive behavior therapy.   I. Title.
   BF637.P36D79 2010
   158'.3–dc22   2010009498

ISBN: 978–0–415–58684–9 (hbk)
ISBN: 978–0–415–58685–6 (pbk)

Dedication

To Kristene Doyle and Ray DiGiuseppe.

Contents

Introduction

Life Coaching is a practice designed to help clients to identify and achieve their personal objectives. It is generally a present-centred and future-focused method where coach and client work together in a collaborative way in the pursuit of the client's goals. While life coaches distinguish themselves from therapists (particularly those who help clients deal with conflicts rooted in the past), there are times in life coaching where the client gets stuck because she (in this case) experiences an emotional problem that is not easily resolved by the coach's standard interventions.

As such, if you, as a life coach, are going to offer your clients a comprehensive service, it is important that (1) you have a working knowledge of common emotional problems that serve as obstacles to client goal achievement; (2) you understand what constitutes healthy alternatives to these emotional problems, and (3) you have a framework for helping your clients to deal with these emotional problems in a constructive way so that they can get on with the business of working towards realizing their personal objectives.

However, having said this, it is useful to remember that your basic goal as a life coach is to help your client to identify, pursue and ultimately achieve her personal life objectives and not to help her with her emotional problems *per se* – that is the role of the psychotherapist or counsellor. The position that I take in this book is that you should only deal with your client's emotional problem when it serves as a specific obstacle to her pursuing her personal objectives because she has become stuck in an unhealthy way of responding to the adversity and she cannot bypass the problem sufficiently to pursue her coaching goals. If your client has many such emotional problems, then you should refer her to a psychotherapist or counsellor to deal with these emotional problems sufficiently so that she can then engage in life coaching productively.[1]

I have three goals in writing this book. First, I will outline the central role played by beliefs in explaining your clients' disturbed and constructive responses to adversities.

---

[1] See Buckley & Buckley (2006) for a full discussion of how to recognize and manage psychological issues in coaching.

Second, I will provide for you a working knowledge of common emotional problems that you are likely to encounter in the course of your career as a life coach and an understanding of what constitutes healthy alternatives to these emotional problems. Third, I present a step-by-step guide to dealing with your clients' emotional problems when these problems explain why your clients become stuck in the coaching process. This guide is based on the insights of a therapeutic tradition known as cognitive behaviour therapy (CBT) and particularly on the ideas of Dr. Albert Ellis (1913–2007), the founder of rational emotive behaviour therapy, a distinctive approach within the CBT tradition. When referring to the approach that underpins this book, I will speak of rational-emotive and cognitive behaviour therapy (RECBT).

This book is best considered as a companion rather than a training course. If you wish to train in RECBT, please refer to www.albertellisinstitute.org for relevant information.

Why RECBT is suited to the practice of life coaching

RECBT is, in some respects, ideally suited to the practice of life coaching for a number of reasons.

- It is an active-directive approach.
- It adopts a present-centred and future-focused time focus, but does not neglect the past when it is important for the client to discuss the past.
- It enables you to engage your client quickly in the process of identifying and dealing with her emotional problem.
- It encourages you to be explicit with your client concerning what you plan to do and encourages her to give her informed consent.
- It helps your client to stay focused.
- It encourages your client to be as specific as possible.
- It urges you to interrupt your client when appropriate, but do so with tact.
- It alerts you to the importance of making sure that your client answers the questions you ask her.
- It encourages you to give your client time to answer your questions.

- It stresses the importance of helping your client to identify and respond to your client's doubts, reservations and objections including those that may be expressed non-verbally.
- It urges you to check out your client's understanding of your substantive points.

Why deal with problematic emotions in life coaching?

In my experience using RECBT as a coach and counsellor, I have found that clients present with one or more of eight common emotional problems that, when clients cannot deal with them on their own, serve as major obstacles to them pursuing their personal objectives. These are: anxiety, depression, shame, guilt, hurt, problematic anger, problematic jealousy and problematic envy. As you will presently see, clients experience these problematic emotions when they encounter negative life events or, what I will call in this guide, adversities. Although you may be tempted as a coach to bypass these problematic emotions and help your clients, in the first instance, to change these adversities, you will find that if you take this stance it will not be terribly effective. This is because problematic emotions, if not dealt with, will usually have a negative impact on your clients' attempts to change these adversities. So, in RECBT, we argue that, most of the time, the most effective long-term strategy in dealing with the presence of clients' emotional problems is to help your clients to address them before encouraging them to change the adversities about which they have the emotional problem, if, indeed, the adversity can be changed. If the adversities cannot be change then the fact that you have helped your clients to deal with emotional problems means that they will be better placed to move on with achieving their personal objectives then if their emotional problems were in place.

However, it is important to stress that in RECBT not all negative emotions are considered problematic and serve as obstacles to the pursuit of personal objectives. Some negative emotions represent constructive responses to life's adversities and help people both to process what has happened to them and to deal with the adversities as productively as they can before either resuming the pursuit of their personal objectives or setting new goals. An understanding of what underlies these problematic and constructive negative emotions is crucial if you are to use RECBT constructively in the course of your life coaching practice and I begin the book, in Part 1, with a presentation of RECBT's position on this point. But first a word of caution about the step-by-step guide presented in Part 3.

The step-by-step guide: a word of caution

If you know anything about jazz, you will know that before you can skilfully improvise on your chosen instrument, you will need to play it properly. This requires you to play and learn musical scales and chords. When you have done this, your improvisation will be based on a sound foundation. The same is true when learning how to practise RECBT well. The steps I will present in this step-by-step guide represent roughly the order that you need to practise them with your clients and you need to learn this sequence before you can improvise with deftness and skill. Once you have done so, avoid using the steps stiltedly and in an overly formalized way, although you will tend to practise RECBT in this way while you are learning the steps. In a nutshell, you need to avoid two errors:

- do not improvise until you have learned how to use the steps in the guide, and
- do not be overly formal and stilted in your use of the steps when you are ready to improvise.

Part 1

The central role played by beliefs in understanding your clients' problematic and constructive negative emotions

RECBT theory is based on an old dictum attributed to the Stoic philosopher, Epictetus, which can be summed up in the phrase: People are disturbed not by things, but by their views of things. This clearly shows the importance of cognitive factors in emotional problems. Albert Ellis, the founder of rational emotive behaviour therapy, developed this point to help us distinguish between negative emotions that are problematic and those that are constructive. Ellis's position can be summarized as follows.

- People experience problematic negative emotions about life's adversities when they hold rigid and extreme beliefs about these adversities.
- People experience constructive negative emotions about life's adversities when they hold flexible and non-extreme beliefs about these adversities.

As you can see from the above, RECBT theory holds that the beliefs that we hold about the adversities that we face are central to the way we respond emotionally to these adversities. In addition, these beliefs also determine how we respond behaviourally to these adversities and how we subsequently think about them, as we will presently see.

In order to help your clients deal with the emotionally based obstacles to their personal objectives, it is important that you understand the role that beliefs play in emotional disturbance and in emotional health. I will begin by outlining the beliefs that underpin emotional disturbance that are known in RECBT as irrational beliefs.

Understanding irrational beliefs

In explaining the role that irrational beliefs play in your clients' emotional problems, I will illustrate my points by discussing the case of Linda who sought life coaching because she was not being challenged in life. I helped her to set a number of goals that she prioritized and then began to take action on. Soon after, she failed to get a promotion at work that she had been promised

> by her boss. This adversity constituted a potential obstacle to her working towards her personal objectives.

In RECBT, irrational beliefs are irrational because they are: (1) false, (2) illogical, and (3) unconstructive. There are four such beliefs that you need to understand; these are rigid beliefs, awfulizing beliefs, discomfort intolerance beliefs and depreciation beliefs.

Rigid beliefs

When your client experiences an adversity – which is usually a negative event of some kind that serves as a potential obstacle to that person pursuing her personal goal – she will healthily have a preference that this adversity did not happen. However, when she holds a rigid belief about the existence of the adversity, she transforms this preference into a rigid belief (e.g. 'I would prefer that this adversity did not happen and therefore it absolutely should not have done so').

> When Linda did not get her promised promotion her rigid belief was: 'My boss absolutely should have kept his promise to promote me'.

While rigid beliefs are based on a person's preferences, they are often expressed without the preference being made explicit. Thus instead of Linda saying: 'I want my boss to have kept his promise to promote me and therefore he absolutely should have done so', she says: 'My boss absolutely should have kept his promise to promote me'.

Your clients can hold rigid beliefs about themselves, other people and/or life conditions and these beliefs can be expressed using the following words: 'must', 'demand', 'absolutely should', 'have to', 'got to', to name but a few.

In RECBT theory, rigid beliefs are at the very heart of

your clients' emotional problems and three other irrational beliefs are derived from them which I will now discuss.

The three extreme beliefs: awfulizing, discomfort intolerance and depreciation beliefs

In RECBT, three major extreme, irrational beliefs are deemed to stem from rigid beliefs. These are:

- awfulizing beliefs
- discomfort intolerance beliefs, and
- depreciation beliefs.

Like rigid beliefs, these three extreme beliefs are deemed to be irrational because they are: (1) false, (2) illogical, and (3) unconstructive.

I will discuss these extreme beliefs one at a time.

Awfulizing beliefs

When your client holds a rigid belief about an adversity, she will tend to hold an extreme awfulizing belief about this adversity as well. This belief is extreme in the sense that your client believes, *at the time*, one or more of the following:

1 Nothing could be worse
2 The event in question is worse than 100% bad, and
3 No good could possibly come from this bad event.

When your client experiences an adversity, she will healthily evaluate this adversity negatively. However, when she holds an extreme awfulizing belief about the existence of the adversity, she transforms this negative evaluation into an awfulizing belief (e.g. 'It is bad that this adversity did happen and therefore it is awful that it did').

> When Linda did not get her promised promotion her extreme awfulizing belief was: 'It is awful that my boss absolutely did not keep his promise to promote me'.

While extreme awfulizing beliefs are based on a person's negative evaluations, they are often expressed without the negative evaluations being made explicit. Thus instead of Linda saying: 'It is bad that my boss did not keep his promise to promote me and therefore it is terrible that he did not do so', she says: 'It is terrible that my boss did not keep his promise to promote me'.

Your clients express extreme awfulizing beliefs using the following words: 'it is terrible that . . .', 'It is awful that . . .' 'It is the end of the world that . . .' to name but a few.

Discomfort intolerance beliefs

When your client holds a rigid belief about an adversity, she will tend to hold an extreme discomfort intolerance belief about this adversity as well. This belief is extreme in the sense that your client believes, *at the time*, one or more of the following:

1 I will die or disintegrate if the adversity continues to exist
2 I will lose the capacity to experience happiness if the adversity continues to exist.

When your client experiences an adversity, she will healthily consider it to be a struggle to tolerate this adversity. However, when she holds an extreme discomfort intolerance belief about the existence of the adversity, she transforms this sense of struggle into a discomfort intolerance belief (e.g. 'It is a struggle for me to put up with the adversity and therefore I can't tolerate it').

When Linda did not get her promised promotion her extreme discomfort intolerance belief was: 'I can't tolerate the fact that my boss did not keep his promise to promote me'.

While extreme discomfort intolerance beliefs are based on a person's sense of struggle, they are often expressed without this sense being made explicit. Thus, instead of Linda saying: 'It is a struggle for me to put up with my boss not keeping his promise to promote me and therefore I can't tolerate it', she says: 'I can't tolerate the fact that my boss did not keep his promise to promote me'.

Your clients express extreme discomfort tolerance beliefs using the following words: 'I can't stand it ...', 'I can't tolerate it ...' 'It is unbearable ...', to name but a few.

Depreciation beliefs

When your client holds a rigid belief about an adversity, she will tend to hold an extreme depreciation belief in relation to this adversity. The target of the depreciation belief depends on who or what your client holds responsible for the adversity. Thus, if the client holds herself responsible for the adversity, she will hold a self-depreciation belief, if she holds another or others responsible for the adversity, she will hold an other-depreciation belief and if she holds life responsible for the adversity, she will hold a life-depreciation belief.

A depreciation belief is extreme in the sense that your client believes, *at the time*, one or more of the following:

1 a person (self or other) can legitimately be given a single global rating that defines their essence and the worth of a person is dependent upon conditions that change (e.g. my worth goes up when I do well and goes down when I don't do well)
2 the world can legitimately be given a single rating that defines its essential nature and that the value of the world varies according to what happens within it (e.g. the value of the world goes up when something fair occurs and goes down when something unfair happens)
3 a person can be rated on the basis of one of his or her aspects and the world can be rated on the basis of one of its aspects.

When your client experiences an adversity, she will focus on this and healthily evaluate the relevant aspect negatively. However, when she holds an extreme depreciation belief about the existence of the adversity, she transforms this negative-aspect evaluation into a global negative evaluation of self, other or life depending on who or what your client holds responsible for the adversity (e.g. 'It is bad I brought about the adversity and therefore I am a bad person for doing so').

When Linda did not get her promised promotion her extreme other depreciation belief was: 'My boss is a bad person for failing to keep his promise to promote me'.

While extreme depreciation beliefs are based on a person's negative evaluations, they are often expressed without the negative evaluations being made explicit. Thus instead of Linda saying: 'It is bad that my boss did not keep his promise to promote me and therefore he is a bad person for not doing so', she says: 'My boss is a bad person for failing to keep his promise to promote me'.

It is important to note that when your clients hold depreciation beliefs, they are assigning a global negative evaluation to self, to others or to life and that these ratings are likely to vary according to the presence or absence of the adversities in question. Thus, Linda may believe that her boss is a bad person for failing to keep his promise to promote her and that he is a good person if he kept his promise. It is also important to note that global evaluations occur on a continuum. Thus, Linda may not believe that her boss is a bad person for failing to keep his promise but that he is less worthy for doing so. The latter is still an other-depreciation belief even though Linda does not use the end-point of the global evaluation continuum since she still assigns her boss a global negative evaluation.

Understanding rational beliefs

In explaining the role that rational beliefs play in your clients' healthy responses to obstacles to the pursuit of their personal objectives, I will again illustrate my points by discussing the case of Linda who sought life coaching because she was not being challenged in life. Remember that I helped her to set a number of personal objectives that she prioritized and then began to take action on. Soon after, she failed to get promotion at work that had been promised to her by her boss. This adversity constituted a potential obstacle to her working towards her personal objectives. In the previous section, I explained how Linda converted this potential obstacle into an actual one largely because of the irrational beliefs that she held about the obstacle. In this section, I will assume that Linda responded constructively to the potential obstacle, which enabled her to resume the pursuit of her personal objectives. In doing so, I will highlight the rational beliefs that were the foundation of this healthy response.

In RECBT, rational beliefs are rational because they are: (1) true, (2) logical, and (3) constructive. There are four such beliefs that you need to understand; these are flexible beliefs, non-awfulizing beliefs, discomfort tolerance beliefs and acceptance beliefs.

Flexible beliefs

When your client experiences an adversity – which, as I said earlier, is usually a negative event of some kind that serves as a potential obstacle to that person pursuing her personal goal – she will healthily have a preference that this adversity did not happen. However, in order for the person not to transform that preference into a rigid belief about the adversity and thus to keep the belief flexible, she needs to negate any implicit demand that she might be making (e.g. 'I would prefer that this adversity did not happen, but that does not mean that it must not happen').

When Linda did not get her promised promotion her flexible belief was: 'I would have much preferred my boss to have kept his promise to promote me, but he does not have to do what I want'.

When a person expresses her preferences without explicitly negating her demand (e.g. 'I would have much preferred my boss to have kept his promise to promote me'), it is easy to conclude that the person is holding a flexible belief. However, the only way to know for certain that the person's belief is flexible or rigid is to consider whether or not the demand is explicitly negated. Thus, Linda could begin with her preference (i.e. 'I would have much preferred my boss to have kept his promise to promote me . . .') and easily transform this into a rigid belief (i.e. '. . . and therefore he absolutely should have done so').

Thus, the only way to say with certainty that a person's belief is flexible is when the person begins with their preference (e.g. 'I would have much preferred my boss to have kept his promise to promote me . . .') and then explicitly negates any implicit demand (e.g. '. . . but he does not have to do what I want').

Your clients can hold flexible beliefs about themselves, other people and/or life conditions and these beliefs can be expressed using the following words: 'want', 'prefer', 'preferably should', 'it would be better', to name but a few. However, as discussed above, for these beliefs to be properly regarded as flexible, implicit demands need to be explicitly negated (e.g. 'but it does not have to be the way I want it to be'; 'but there is no reason why it has to be; 'but it is not absolutely necessary').

In RECBT theory, flexible beliefs are at the very heart of your clients' constructive responses to adversity and three other rational beliefs, termed non-extreme beliefs, are derived from them and I will now discuss these.

The three non-extreme beliefs: non-awfulizing, discomfort tolerance and depreciation beliefs

In RECBT, three major non-extreme rational beliefs are deemed to stem from flexible beliefs. These are:

- non-awfulizing beliefs
- discomfort tolerance beliefs, and
- acceptance beliefs.

Like flexible beliefs, these three non-extreme beliefs are deemed to be rational because they are: (1) true, (2) logical, and (3) constructive.

I will discuss these non-extreme beliefs one at a time.

Non-awfulizing beliefs

When your client holds a flexible belief about an adversity, she will tend to hold a non-extreme non-awfulizing belief about this adversity as well. This belief is non-extreme in the sense that your client believes, *at the time*, one or more of the following:

1 things could always be worse
2 the event in question is less than 100% bad, and
3 good could come from this bad event.

When your client experiences an adversity, she will healthily evaluate this adversity negatively. However, in order for the person not to transform this negative evaluation into an extreme awfulizing belief about the adversity and thus to keep the belief non-extreme, she needs to negate any sense of awfulizing (e.g. 'It is bad that this adversity happened, but not awful').

> When Linda did not get her promised promotion her non-extreme non-awfulizing belief was: 'It is bad that my boss did not keep his promise to promote me, but not awful'.

When a person expresses her non-awfulizing belief without

explicitly negating the awfulizing component (e.g. 'It is bad that my boss did not keep his promise to promote me'), it is easy to conclude that the person is holding a non-awfulizing belief. However, the only way to know for certain that the person's belief is a non-extreme non-awfulizing one is to consider whether or not the awfulizing component is negated. Thus, Linda could begin with her negative evaluation (i.e. 'It is bad that my boss did not keep his promise to promote me . . .') and easily transform this into an extreme awfulizing belief (i.e. '. . . and therefore it is awful').

Thus, the only way to say with certainty that a person's belief is a non-extreme non-awfulizing one is when the person begins with their negative evaluation (e.g. 'It is bad that my boss did not keep his promise to promote me . . .') and then explicitly negate any implicit awfulizing component (e.g. '. . . but it isn't awful').

Your clients can hold non-extreme non-awfulizing beliefs with reference to themselves, other people and/or life conditions and these beliefs can be expressed using the following words: 'it is bad that . . .', 'it is unfortunate that . . .', to name but two. However, as discussed above, for these beliefs to be properly regarded as non-extreme the implicit awfulizing components need to be explicitly negated (e.g. '. . . but it is not awful', 'but it is not the end of the world').

Discomfort tolerance beliefs

When your client holds a flexible belief about an adversity, she will tend to hold a non-extreme discomfort tolerance belief about her ability to withstand this adversity as well. This belief is non-extreme in the sense that your client believes, *at the time*, one or more of the following:

1 I will struggle if the discomfort continues to exist, but I will neither die nor disintegrate
2 I will not lose the capacity to experience happiness if the discomfort continues to exist, although this capacity will be temporarily diminished, and
3 The discomfort is worth tolerating.

When your client experiences an adversity, she will healthily think that it is a struggle for her to withstand this adversity. However, in order for the person not to transform this healthy sense of struggle into an extreme discomfort intolerance belief in relation to the adversity and thus to keep the belief non-extreme, she needs to both negate any sense of being unable to tolerate the discomfort of facing the adversity, and indicate that it is in her interests to withstand the adversity (e.g. 'It is difficult for me to tolerate this adversity, but I can tolerate it and it is worth it to me to do so').

> When Linda did not get her promised promotion her extreme discomfort tolerance belief was: 'It is a struggle for me to tolerate the fact that my boss did not keep his promise to promote me, but I can tolerate this and it is worth it to me to do so'.

When a person expresses her discomfort tolerance belief without explicitly negating the intolerance component (e.g. 'It is a struggle for me to tolerate the fact that my boss did not keep his promise to promote me'), it is easy to conclude that the person is holding a discomfort tolerance belief. However, the only way to know for certain that the person's belief is a non-extreme discomfort tolerance one is to consider whether or not (1) the intolerance component is negated, and (2) the 'worth it' component is asserted. Thus, Linda could begin with her sense of struggle (i.e. 'It is a struggle for me to tolerate the fact that my boss did not keep his promise to promote me ...') and easily transform this into an extreme discomfort intolerance belief (i.e. '... and therefore I can't tolerate it').

Thus, the only way to say with certainty that a person's belief is a non-extreme discomfort tolerance one is when the person:

- begins with their sense of struggle (e.g. 'It is a struggle for me to tolerate the fact that my boss did not keep his promise to promote me ...')

- explicitly negates any implicit intolerance component (e.g. '. . . but I can tolerate this . . .'), and
- asserts the 'worth it' component (e.g. '. . . and it is worth it to me to do so').

Your clients can hold non-extreme discomfort tolerance beliefs with reference to themselves, other people and/or life conditions and these beliefs can be expressed using the following words: 'I can tolerate this', 'I can bear it', 'I can stand it' to name but a few. However, as discussed above, for these beliefs to be properly regarded as discomfort tolerance beliefs, the 'worth it' component needs to be made explicit (e.g. 'and it is worth it to me to do so'). Otherwise, the person may recognize theoretically that she can tolerate discomfort, but choose not to do so because she cannot see that it is in her best interests to do so.

Acceptance beliefs

When your client holds a flexible belief about an adversity, she will tend to hold a non-extreme acceptance belief in relation to this adversity. The target of the acceptance belief depends on who or what your client holds responsible for the adversity. Thus, if the client holds herself responsible for the adversity, she will hold a self-acceptance belief, if she holds another or others responsible for the adversity, she will hold an other-acceptance belief and if she holds life responsible for the adversity, she will hold a life-acceptance belief.

An acceptance belief is non-extreme in the sense that your client believes, *at the time*, one or more of the following:

1 A person cannot legitimately be given a single global rating that defines their essence and their worth, as far as they have it, is not dependent upon conditions that change (e.g. my worth stays the same whether or not I do well)
2 The world cannot legitimately be given a single rating that defines its essential nature and that the value of the world does not vary according to what happens within it (e.g. the value of the world stays the same whether fairness exists at any given time or not)
3 It makes sense to rate discrete aspects of a person and of

the world, but it does not make sense to rate a person or the world on the basis of these discrete aspects.

When your client experiences an adversity, she will focus on this and healthily evaluate the relevant aspect negatively. As mentioned above, this aspect may be to do with oneself, another person or persons or life conditions. However, in order for the person not to transform this negative evaluation into an extreme depreciation belief about the adversity and thus to keep the belief non-extreme, she needs to negate any sense of depreciation (e.g. 'It is bad that I brought about this adversity, but I am fallible for doing so and not a bad person').

> When Linda did not get her promised promotion her non-extreme other-acceptance belief was: 'It is bad that my boss failed to keep his promise to promote me, but he is not a bad person for failing to do so. Rather, he is a fallible, unrateable human being who did the wrong thing'.

When a person expresses her acceptance belief while negating the depreciation component (e.g. 'It is bad that my boss failed to keep his promise to promote me, but he is not a bad person for failing to do so . . .'), it is easy to conclude that the person is holding an acceptance belief (in this case an other-acceptance belief. However, the only way to know for certain that the person's belief is a non-extreme, acceptance one is to consider whether or not (1) the depreciation component is negated, and (2) the acceptance component is asserted. Thus, Linda could begin with negating the other-depreciation component (i.e. 'It is bad that my boss failed to keep his promise to promote me, but he is not a bad person for failing to do so . . .') and easily transform this into an extreme depreciation component whereby the worth of the person still varies (e.g. '. . . however, he would be worthier if he kept his promise than if he broke it).

Thus, the only way to say with certainty that a person's belief is a non-extreme acceptance one is when the person:

- begins with negatively evaluating the relevant aspect (e.g. 'It is bad that my boss failed to keep his promise to promote me . . .')
- explicitly negates any implicit depreciation component (e.g. '. . . but he is not a bad person for failing to do so . . .'), and
- asserts the 'acceptance' component (e.g. '. . . rather, he is a fallible, unrateable human being who did the wrong thing').

This is why Albert Ellis (2005) referred to acceptance beliefs as *unconditional* acceptance beliefs because, in this case for example, Linda's boss is accepted unconditionally as a fallible, unrateable person whose worth (if he can be said to have it) does not change in the light of his changing behaviour.

Your clients can hold non-extreme acceptance beliefs with reference to themselves, other people and/or life conditions. When acceptance beliefs refer to a person (self or others), the following words (or synonyms) should be used: 'I am (or you are) fallible, unrateable, complex and in flux'. If the concept of worth is to be used, then it should be made clear that such 'worth' is a given about the person and does not change in his or her lifetime. Thus the unconditional aspect of self-acceptance and other-acceptance should preferably be emphasized here.

When acceptance beliefs refer to life, the following words (or synonyms) should be used: 'Life is a complex mixture of good, bad and neutral aspects, too complex to be given a single rating'. Again, if the concept of worth is to be used with respect to life, then it should be made clear once more that such 'worth' is a given about life and does not change according to changing circumstances. The unconditional aspect of life-acceptance should again preferably be emphasized here.

Part 2

Understanding your clients' common emotional problems and their healthy alternatives

The 'situational ABC' framework

In the previous part of this book, I discussed irrational beliefs and their rational alternatives. I made the point that irrational beliefs are at the core of your clients' disturbed responses to life's adversities and that rational beliefs are at the core of their constructive responses to the same negative events. RECBT outlines a 'situational ABC' framework that I will use in helping you to understand your clients' emotional problems and their healthy alternatives. In this framework, 'A' stands for the Adversity that your client is facing or thinks she is facing, 'B' stands for the Beliefs that your client holds about this actual or perceived adversity and 'C' stands for the Consequences of holding these beliefs. These consequences are emotional, behavioural and cognitive in nature. In this part of the book, I will consider both problematic and constructive emotional responses to adversities before showing how you can help your clients deal effectively with the former and experience the latter in Parts 3 and 4 of the book.

It is a fundamental view of RECBT theory that when your client experiences an adversity it is constructive for her to experience a healthy negative emotion (which I refer to as an HNE) since doing so enables her to process the experience emotionally, make sense of what has happened to her and move on with her life. You only need to help your client deal with a life adversity in life coaching when she experiences an unhealthy negative emotion (known as an UNE) in response to this adversity and gets stuck as a result. This latter point is very important. If your client first experiences a problematic or unhealthy emotion about an adversity, but then regroups and deals with it effectively later, then you do not need to intervene since your client has got herself back on the path of working towards her personal objectives. However, if she has responded to an adversity with a problematic negative emotion, remains stuck in this mode and cannot bypass it, then she requires your intervention.

'A' stands for adversity

Earlier, I mentioned the work of Albert Ellis, the founder of rational emotive behaviour therapy, who distinguished carefully between irrational and rational beliefs. When understanding what constitutes an adversity for your client, we need to draw on the work of another giant in the field of cognitive behaviour therapy (CBT), Aaron T. Beck, who introduced the concept of the personal domain (Beck, 1976).

Beck thought of the personal domain as a kind of psychological space that contains anything that the person deems to be personally valuable. An adversity can thus be seen as a negative event that has a particular relation to the person's personal domain as perceived by the person herself. In my view there are two major parts of the personal domain: that which relates to the person's sense of worth or ego (the ego part of the domain) and that which relates to those things that the person values, which do not relate to the person's sense of worth or ego (the non-ego part of the domain). Thus, as we shall presently see, a person may feel anxiety or concerned when she perceives a threat to either the ego or non-ego part of her personal domain.

As this example shows, an adversity on its own at 'A' does not tell us whether the person's emotional response to it is healthy or unhealthy (we need to know whether the person holds rational or irrational beliefs to know that). However, when we know the theme of an adversity (e.g. threat) we at least know that the person will either experience an unhealthy negative emotion (e.g. anxiety in the case of threat) or a healthy negative emotion (e.g. concern in the case of threat). Later in this Part (pp. 28–47) I will discuss eight pairs of emotions and show how they relate to different adversity themes.

'C' stands for consequences

'C' in the 'ABC' framework stands for the consequences that the person experiences when she holds a belief (at 'B') about the adversity (at 'A'). There are three major sets of consequences that we need to consider: emotional consequences, behavioural consequences and thinking consequences. We already know that the emotional consequence of irrational beliefs about an adversity is likely to be negative and problematic (i.e. a UNE). Whereas when the person holds a set of rational beliefs about the same adversity, then her emotion is likely to be negative and constructive (i.e. an HNE).

In similar vein, when the person holds a set of irrational beliefs about the adversity her behavioural consequences will be unconstructive (i.e. she is likely to behave in an unconstructive way) and her thinking consequences will be unconstructive (i.e. she will subsequently think in a highly distorted and negative manner). When she experiences such unconstructive behavioural and thinking consequences, these combined with the associated unhealthy emotional consequences will lead the person to become stuck. She will require your help to refocus on her coaching goals if she is stuck and if she cannot bypass her emotional problem sufficiently to pursue these goals.

However, when the person holds a set of rational beliefs about the adversity, her behavioural consequences will be constructive (i.e. she is likely to behave in a constructive way) and her thinking consequences will be constructive (i.e. she will subsequently think in a realistic and balanced manner). Together with her healthy emotional response her subsequent behaviour and thinking will enable her to process the adversity effectively and move on.

I will bring all these 'ABC' components together in detailing the eight common emotional problems that you will encounter in life coaching and their healthy alternatives. In doing so, I will discuss the factors involved in both the emotional problem and its healthy alternative and will provide you with a tabular summary of the differences between unhealthy negative emotions (UNEs) and healthy negative emotions (HNEs).

Before I begin, I want to make an important observation on emotions and the labels we give to them.

Emotions and the labels we give to them

A central plank of RECBT theory of emotional problems and their solutions is that when your client faces an adversity – either one that can be objectively verified or one that she interprets personally as an adversity – then she is bound to experience a negative emotion. When she is bogged down with this emotional response accompanied by associated behavioural and thinking responses, then this emotion is likely to be negative in tone and unhealthy in consequence. We call these emotions unhealthy negative emotions (or UNEs) in RECBT theory.

Alternatively, when your client experiences a negative emotion about this adversity, but is not bogged down by it and can get on with her life, albeit with some difficulty, then this negative emotion will be accompanied by a different set of behavioural and thinking responses that aid recovery. We call these emotions healthy negative emotions (or HNEs) in RECBT theory.

It is important for you to note when I discuss these emotions that we do not, as humans, have a universally agreed and accepted lexicon when it comes to emotions. What appear below are comparisons between pairs of UNEs and HNEs. Please remember throughout what follows that the labels I have given the eight pairs of emotions are my own and should not be uncritically used in coaching practice.

What is important is that when you are working with a client on the emotional problem that she is stuck with, and which serves as an obstacle to her progress towards her personal objectives, that you develop a shared understanding which label you are going to give to her major UNE and to her HNE alternative. You may, of course, use the language that I employ below as a starting off point, but it is good coaching practice to end up with agreed emotional terms that you can both use to differentiate your client's UNE from the HNE, which hopefully comprises her emotional goal that you are going to help her achieve. I discuss this issue from a more practical perspective in Steps 4 (p. 66) and 9 (p. 88) in the guide that appears in Part 3 of this book. With this caveat, let me discuss the eight unhealthy negative emotions

(Dryden, 2009), one of which is very likely to feature in your client's emotional problems, and their eight healthy alternatives. In doing so, I will not cover all possible features of these emotions, just their main features.

Anxiety and concern

As I mentioned above, when your client has an emotional problem where anxiety predominates then the adversity that features at 'A' in the 'ABC' framework will be some kind of threat to her personal domain. This threat may be deemed to be to her self-esteem or broadly speaking to the non-ego domain of her sense of comfort. Albert Ellis (1979, 1980) used the terms 'ego anxiety and discomfort anxiety' to distinguish between these two forms of anxiety.

From an RECBT theoretical perspective, it is important to bear in mind that threat-based adversity does not, on its own, bring about your client's anxiety. Rather, it is the rigid and extreme beliefs that she holds about this adversity that are at the core of her anxiety response. Aside from the emotional part of this response when your client is anxious her behaviour will be dominated by a wish to escape from this threat as quickly as possible or seek safety if she cannot escape physically from it. In addition, her subsequent thinking will exaggerate the nature of the threat and its consequences/implications and because these thoughts (in words or in images) will be vivid, and backed up by increased anxious feeling your client may well think that they have a predictive quality. In other words, your client will operate on the principle at this point that 'If I think it, then it is likely to happen'.

Your coaching goal is to help your client deal with this threat in a healthier manner so that she can get 'unstuck' and move on with her life, including resuming the work that she had started with you pursuing her personal objectives. In RECBT theory, we regard concern (or whatever emotional term you and your client have agreed to use) as the healthy alternative to anxiety in dealing with a threat-based adversity.

Concern, from an RECBT theoretical perspective, stems

from a set of flexible and non-extreme beliefs about threat-based adversity. Aside from the emotional part of this response when your client is concerned, but not anxious, she will be inclined, behaviourally, to face up to and deal with the threat rather than escape from it. Her subsequent thinking will be realistic and balanced in nature rather than highly distorted and skewed as in anxiety.

If you can help your client to develop a flexible and non-extreme attitude towards the threat, and encourage her to act and think in ways that are consistent with her rational belief, then you will not only help her to be healthily concerned rather than anxious about her threat-based adversity, you will help her to get unstuck and move on with her life including resuming her coaching work towards her personal objectives. Table 1 reviews the major features of anxiety and concern. You will see from the table that the 'A' is the same for both emotions, but the 'B' and 'C' are different. This is true for all eight pairs of emotions that I will discuss in this part of the book.

Depression[1] and sadness

When your client has an emotional problem where depression predominates then the adversity that features at 'A' in the 'ABC' framework will be some kind of loss or failure within your client's personal domain. This loss or failure may again be deemed to be to her self-esteem or broadly speaking to the non-ego domain of her sense of comfort.

Again from an RECBT theoretical perspective, it is important to bear in mind that loss-based or failure-based adversity does not, on its own, bring about your client's depression. Rather, it is the rigid and extreme beliefs

---

[1] It is important for you to note that I am talking about non-clinical depression here. Clinical depression is characterised by a number of biological features such as insomnia, loss of appetite, loss of libido and suicidal ideation. You should not attempt to help your client if she is experiencing this kind of depression. Rather, you should effect a referral to the client's general practitioner in the first instance.

Table 1 Anxiety and Concern

Adversity at 'A'	Belief at 'B'	Emotion at 'C'	Behaviour at 'C'	Subsequent thinking at 'C'
Threat to personal domain	Irrational	Anxiety	• You withdraw physically from the threat • You withdraw mentally from the threat • You ward off the threat (e.g. by superstitious behaviour) • You tranquillize your feelings • You seek reassurance	• You overestimate the probability of the threat occurring • You underestimate your ability to cope with the threat • You create an even more negative threat in your mind • You have more task-irrelevant thoughts than in concern
Threat to personal domain	Rational	Concern	• You face up to the threat • You deal with the threat constructively • You take constructive action to reduce/minimize the risk or danger	• You are realistic about the probability of the threat occurring • You view the threat realistically • You realistically appraise your ability to cope with the threat • You do not create an even more negative threat in your mind • You have more task-relevant thoughts than in anxiety

that she holds about this adversity that are at the core of her depressive response. Aside from the emotional part of this response when your client is depressed her behaviour will be dominated by a wish to withdraw into herself and away from what was previously experienced as enjoyable. There is a general shutting down of ordinary responsiveness. In addition, her subsequent thinking will be characterized by memories of past losses or failures and a general sense of helplessness and, in extreme cases, of depression and hopelessness.

Aaron T. Beck, who coined the term 'personal domain' (Beck, 1976) has made a useful distinction between autonomy-related depression and sociotropy-related depression.

If your client experiences autonomy-related depression she is depressed about a loss or failure within that part of her domain in which her sense of autonomy, effectiveness, competence is highly prized. Examples of autonomy-related self-beliefs related to depression are: 'I am weak', 'I am defective' and 'I am a failure' and the conditions and the non-ego conditions that your client believes she cannot tolerate include being dependent on others, having one's sense of freedom restrained and being unable to achieve one's valued goals.

On the other hand, if your client experiences sociotropy-related depression she is depressed about a loss or failure within that part of her domain in which her connection to others and how others see her are highly prized. Examples of sociotropy-related self-beliefs related to depression are: 'I am unlovable', 'I am unlikeable' and 'I am worthless' and the non-ego conditions that your client believes she cannot tolerate include not having someone on whom one can depend, being alone and being rejected.

Your coaching goal is again to help your client deal with this loss or failure in a healthier manner so that she can get unstuck and move on with her life, including resuming the work that she had started with you pursuing her personal objectives. In RECBT theory, we regard sadness (or whatever emotional term you and your client have agreed to use) as the healthy alternative to depression in dealing with a loss-based or failure-based adversity.

Sadness is deemed to be the healthy alternative to depression (although the important point here is the term you and your client have agreed to use as the healthy alternative to depression) and from an RECBT theoretical perspective, it stems from a set of flexible and non-extreme beliefs about loss-based or failure-based adversity. Aside from the emotional part of this response when your client is sad, but not depressed, she will be inclined, behaviourally, to stay connected to the world rather than withdraw from it. Her subsequent thinking will be realistic and balanced in nature rather than highly distorted and skewed as in depression.

If you can help your client to develop a flexible and non-extreme attitude towards the loss or failure, and encourage her to act and think in ways that are consistent with her rational belief, then you will not only help her to be healthily sad rather than depressed about her loss-based or failure-based adversity, you will help her to get unstuck and move on with her life including resuming her coaching work towards her personal objectives. Table 2 reviews the major features of depression and sadness.

Guilt and remorse

When your client has an emotional problem where guilt predominates then the adversity that features at 'A' in the 'ABC' framework will be a violation of her moral code, a failure to live up to her moral code or where the person has hurt the feelings of another person or persons. As with other emotions, a rigid belief and an extreme self-belief mediate between the above themes at 'A' and the emotion of guilt at 'C'. Indeed, guilt is one of only two UNEs that is based exclusively on self-rating (shame is the other). In guilt, the self-rating concerns one's badness.

Aside from the emotional part of this response when your client feels guilt, her behaviour will be dominated by a wish to beg for forgiveness along with the sense that one does not deserve to be forgiven. In addition, her subsequent thinking will exaggerate the threat of retribution from others or by some deity.

Table 2 Depression and Sadness

Adversity at 'A'	Belief at 'B'	Emotion at 'C'	Behaviour at 'C'	Subsequent thinking at 'C'
• Loss (with implications for future) • Failure	Irrational	Depression	• You withdraw from reinforcements • You withdraw into yourself • You create an environment consistent with your depressed feelings • You attempt to terminate feelings of depression in self-destructive ways	• You see only negative aspects of the loss or failure • You think of other losses and failures that you have experienced • You think you are unable to help yourself (helplessness) • You only see pain and blackness in the future (hopelessness)
• Loss (with implications for future) • Failure	Rational	Sadness	• You seek out reinforcements after a period of mourning • You express your feelings about the loss or failure and talk about these to significant others	• You are able to recognize both negative and positive aspects of the loss or failure • You think you are able to help youself • You look to the future with hope

Remorse is, from an RECBT theoretical perspective, deemed to be the healthy alternative to guilt (although again the important issue here is the term you and your client have agreed to use as the healthy alternative to guilt). It stems from a set of flexible and non-extreme beliefs about doing the wrong thing, failing to do the right thing or hurting someone. Aside from the emotional part of this response when your client feels remorse, rather than guilt, she will be inclined, behaviourally, to look for forgiveness rather than begging for it, accompanied by the sense that she is worthy of forgiveness. Her subsequent thinking will be realistic and balanced in nature and relate to one being penalized rather than receiving divine or human retribution as in guilt.

As with other emotions, your task is to help your client to develop a flexible and non-extreme attitude towards moral code violations and to encourage her to act and think in ways that are consistent with her rational belief. If she feels remorse rather than guilt she will be able to come to terms with what she did (or failed to do) and resume her coaching work towards her personal objectives. Table 3 reviews the major features of guilt and remorse.

Shame and disappointment

When your client has an emotional problem where shame predominates then the adversity that features at 'A' in the 'ABC' framework will be a drastic falling short of a valued standard perpetrated by herself or by a member of a social group with which your client closely identifies, together with a sense (which may or may not reflect reality) that your client and/or the group involved is being devalued by relevant judging observers. As with other emotions, a rigid belief and an extreme self-belief mediate between the above themes at 'A' and the emotion of shame. In shame, the self-rating concerns one's defectiveness or disgracefulness either as a result of your client's own behaviour or through membership of the 'shamed' social group with whom she identifies

Aside from the emotional part of this response when your client feels shame, her behaviour will be dominated by a

Table 3 Guilt and remorse

Adversity at 'A'	Belief at 'B'	Emotion at 'C'	Behaviour at 'C'	Subsequent thinking at 'C'
• Violation of moral code (sin of commission) • Failure to live up to moral code (sin of omission) • Hurts the feelings of a significant other	Irrational	Guilt	• You escape from the unhealthy pain of guilt in self-defeating ways • You beg forgiveness from the person you wronged • You promise unrealistically that you will not 'sin' again • You punish yourself physically or by deprivation • You defensively disclaim responsibility for wrongdoing • You reject offers of forgiveness	• You assume that you have definitely committed the sin • You assume more personal responsibility than the situation warrants • You assign far less responsibility to others than is warranted • You do not think of mitigating factors • You do not put your behaviour into an overall context • You think that you will receive retribution
• Violation of moral code (sin of commission) • Failure to live up to moral code (sin of omission) • Hurts the feelings of a significant other	Rational	Remorse	• You face up to the healthy pain that accompanies the realization that you have sinned • You ask, but do not beg, for forgiveness • You understand the reasons for wrongdoing and act on your understanding • You atone for the sin by taking a penalty • You make appropriate amends • You do not make excuses for your behaviour or enact other defensive behaviour • You do accept offers of forgiveness	• You take into account all relevant data when judging whether or not you have 'sinned' • You assume an appropriate level of personal responsibility • You assign an appropriate level of responsibility to others • You take into account mitigating factors • You put your behaviour into overall context • You do not think you will receive retribution

wish to disappear from the judgemental gaze of the observing group. In addition, her subsequent thinking will exaggerate the extent of social scorn and exclusion and the perceived implications of such social condemnation.

Disappointment is, from an RECBT theoretical perspective, deemed to be the healthy alternative to shame (although again the important point here is the term you and your client have agreed to use as the healthy alternative to shame). It stems from a set of flexible and non-extreme beliefs about an observed and negatively judged significant falling short of a valued standard by self or closely identified other. Aside from the emotional part of this response when your client feels disappointed, rather than ashamed, she will be inclined, behaviourally, to look at the judging group and engage in a dialogue about the possible reasons for one's behaviour or that of the closely identified other accompanied by the sense that one is not defective or disgraceful as a person. Her subsequent thinking will be realistic and balanced in nature and relate to the broad range of responses from the judging group and the time-limited nature of any social censure or exclusion.

As with other emotions, your task is to help your client to develop a flexible and non-extreme attitude towards drastic falls from 'grace' and to encourage her to act and think in ways that are consistent with her rational belief. If she feels disappointed rather than ashamed she will be able to come to terms with her behaviour or that of the closely identified other and resume her coaching work towards her personal objectives. Table 4 reviews the major features of shame and disappointment.

Hurt and sorrow

When your client has an emotional problem where feelings of hurt predominate then the adversity that features at 'A' in the 'ABC' framework will be a sense of her being let down by a significant other where she considers herself undeserving of such treatment. As with other emotions, a rigid belief and an extreme belief mediate between the above theme at 'A' and the emotion of hurt. In hurt, your

Table 4 Shame and disappointment

Adversity at 'A'	Belief at 'B'	Emotion at 'C'	Behaviour at 'C'	Subsequent thinking at 'C'
• Something shameful has been revealed about you (or a group with whom you identify) by yourself or by others • Acting in a way that falls very short of your ideal • Others will look down on or shun you (or a group with whom you identify)	Irrational	Shame	• You remove yourself from the 'gaze' of others • You isolate yourself from others • You save face by attacking other(s) who have 'shamed' you • You defend your threatened self-esteem in self-defeating ways • You ignore attempts by others to restore social equilibrium	• You overestimate the 'shamefulness' of the information revealed • You overestimate the likelihood that the judging group will notice or be interested in the information • You overestimate the degree of disapproval you (or your reference group) will receive • You overestimate the length of time any disapproval will last
• Something shameful has been revealed about you (or a group with whom you identify) by yourself or by others • Acting in a way that falls very short of your ideal • Others will look down on or shun you (or a group with whom you identify)	Rational	Disappointment	• You continue to participate actively in social interaction • You respond to attempts of others to restore social equilibrium	• You see the information revealed in a compassionate self-accepting context • You are realistic about the likelihood that the judging group will notice or be interested in the information revealed • You are realistic about the degree of disapproval (self or reference group) will receive • You are realistic about the length of time any disapproval will last

client either feels sorry for herself (non-ego hurt) or considers herself worth less as a result of such treatment (ego hurt).

Aside from the emotional part of this response when your client feels hurt, her behaviour will be dominated by a wish to stop communicating directly with the person who she sees as having 'hurt' her. Having said this, your client may well also seek ways of communicating her feelings indirectly to the other, mainly by sulking. In addition, her subsequent thinking will exaggerate the extent of the bad treatment and she will think of ways to make the person suffer.

Sorrow is, from an RECBT theoretical perspective, deemed to be the healthy alternative to hurt (although, as before, the important point here is the term you and your client have agreed to use as the healthy alternative to hurt). It stems from a set of flexible and non-extreme beliefs about undeserved bad treatment from a significant other. Aside from the emotional part of this response when your client feels sorrowful, rather than hurt, she will be inclined, behaviourally, to communicate her feelings of sorrow directly to the other person. Her subsequent thinking will be realistic and balanced in nature and place the person's behaviour into a broader context where humans are not immune from treating one another badly, even those close to them.

As with other emotions, your task is to help your client to develop a flexible and non-extreme attitude towards undeserved, bad treatment from a significant other and to encourage her to act and think in ways that are consistent with her rational belief. If she feels sorrowful rather than hurt, she will be able to come to terms with the behaviour of the other person and resume her coaching work towards her personal objectives. Table 5 reviews the major features of hurt and sorrow.

Problematic anger and constructive anger

When your client has an emotional problem where unhealthy anger predominates then the adversity that features at 'A' in

Table 5 Hurt and Sorrow

Adversity at 'A'	Belief at 'B'	Emotion at 'C'	Behaviour at 'C'	Subsequent thinking at 'C'
Others treat you badly (and you think you do not deserve such treatment)	Irrational	Hurt	• You shut down communication channel with the other • You sulk and make obvious you feel hurt without disclosing details of the matter • You indirectly criticize or punish the other for the offence	• You overestimate the unfairness of the other person's behaviour • You think that the other person does not care for you or is indifferent to you • You see yourself as alone, uncared for or misunderstood • You tend to think of past 'hurts' • You expect the other to make the first move toward repairing the relationship
Others treat you badly (and you think you do not deserve such treatment)	Rational	Sorrow	• You communicate your feelings to the other directly • You influence the other person to act in a fairer manner towards you	• You are realistic about the degree of unfairness in the other person's behaviour • You think that the other person has acted badly rather than as demonstrating lack of caring or indifference • You do not see yourself as alone, uncared for or misunderstood • You are less likely to think of past hurts • You do not think that the other has to make the first move

the 'ABC' framework will be a transgression of one of your client's important rules by self (unhealthy anger at self) or by another (unhealthy anger at self) or an attack on her self-esteem by someone. In this section, I will concentrate on anger at another person or persons. As with other emotions, a rigid belief and an extreme belief mediate between the above theme at 'A' and the emotion of unhealthy anger, although your client will often cling to the idea that the other (in particular) caused her unhealthy anger directly.

Aside from the emotional part of this response when your client feels unhealthy anger, her behaviour will be dominated by a wish to attack the other either physically or psychologically along with a desire to suppress this tendency. When this suppression fails or is bypassed, unhealthy anger is transformed into aggression. In addition, your client's subsequent thinking will exaggerate the malicious intent of the other and she will be preoccupied with thoughts of revenge.

Healthy anger is, from an RECBT theoretical perspective, deemed to be the healthy alternative to unhealthy anger (although, as I have consistently said, the important point here is the term you and your client have agreed to use as the healthy alternative to unhealthy anger). It stems from a set of flexible and non-extreme beliefs about the other transgressing your client's important rule or attacking her self-esteem. Aside from the emotional part of this response when your client feels healthy anger, rather than unhealthy anger, she will be inclined, behaviourally, to communicate her feelings of displeasure directly to the other person from the position of demonstrating acceptance of the other. This is nicely summed up by a quote attributed to Voltaire who was reported to say to someone: 'Sir, I disapprove of what you say, but I will defend to the death your right to say it.' When healthily angry, your client's subsequent thinking will again be realistic and balanced in nature and she will think about how best to assert herself with the other person rather than punish him or her.

As with other emotions, your task is to help your client to develop a flexible and non-extreme attitude towards the other's rule transgressing and self-esteem attacking behaviour. In rule transgression the non-extreme belief will most likely be an other-acceptance belief whereas when the other attacks your client's self-esteem she needs to hold both an other-acceptance belief and a self-acceptance belief. You also need to encourage her to act and think in ways that are consistent with her rational beliefs. If she feels healthily angry rather than unhealthily angry, she will be able to come to terms with the behaviour of the other person and resume her coaching work towards her personal objectives. Table 6 reviews the major features of unhealthy anger and healthy anger.

Problematic jealousy[2] and constructive jealousy

When your client has an emotional problem where unhealthy jealousy predominates then the adversity that features at 'A' in the 'ABC' framework will be an inferred threat to an important relationship with a prized other. As with other emotions, a rigid belief and an extreme belief mediate between the above theme at 'A' and the emotion of unhealthy jealousy. In unhealthy jealousy, your client finds uncertainty about what the person with whom she is involved is doing or thinking intolerable (non-ego features of unhealthy jealousy) and considers herself less worthy than potential rivals to the affections of the other with whom she is involved (ego features of unhealthy jealousy)

Aside from the emotional part of this response when your client feels unhealthily jealous, her behaviour will be dominated by a wish to prevent the other from relating with potential rivals or to monitor the behaviour and thinking of the other person when he in the company of women. In addition, her subsequent thinking will exaggerate the meaning of any contact between the person and her rivals and will elaborate though imagery the threat contained in such contact.

---

[2] If your client has a chronic problem with unhealthy jealousy, she probably requires ongoing therapy rather than time-limited focused help from you on this emotional problem. Only deal with an episode of unhealthy jealousy if your client does NOT have a chronic problem with this emotion.

Table 6 Unhealthy anger and healthy anger

Adversity at 'A'	Belief at 'B'	Emotion at 'C'	Behaviour at 'C'	Subsequent thinking at 'C'
• Frustration • Goal obstruction • Self or other transgresses personal rule • Threat to self-esteem	Irrational	Unhealthy anger	• You attack the other(s) physically • You attack the other(s) verbally • You attack the other(s) passive-aggressively • You displace the attack on to another person, animal or object • You withdraw aggressively • You recruit allies against the other(s)	• You overestimate the extent to which the other(s) acted deliberately • You see malicious intent in the motives of the other(s) • You see yourself as definitely right and the other(s) as definitely wrong • You are unable to see the point of view of the other(s) • You plot to exact revenge
• Frustration • Goal obstruction • Self or other transgresses personal rule • Threat to self-esteem	Rational	Healthy anger	• You assert yourself with the other(s) • You request, but do not demand, behavioural change from the other(s) • You leave an unsatisfactory situation non-aggressively after taking steps to deal with it	• You do not overestimate the extent to which the other(s) acted deliberately • You are able to see the point of view of the other(s) • You do not plot to exact revenge • You do not see malicious intent in the motives of the other(s) • You do not see yourself as definitely right and the other(s) as definitely wrong

Healthy jealousy is, from an RECBT theoretical perspective, deemed to be the healthy alternative to unhealthy jealousy (once again, the important point here is the term you and your client have agreed to use as the healthy alternative to unhealthy jealousy). It stems from a set of flexible and non-extreme beliefs about an inferred threat to your client's relationship with a prized other. Aside from the emotional part of this response when your client feels healthy jealousy, rather than unhealthy jealousy, she will be inclined, behaviourally, to tolerate uncertainty and not check on the activities of the other, for example, and where there is evidence of a threat to her relationship to communicate her concerns directly to the other person. Her subsequent thinking will again be realistic and balanced in nature and will locate the person's behaviour within a non-threatening context. There will also be no mental elaborations of any threatening aspects of contact between the prized person and any rivals. Indeed, in healthy jealousy, others are not deemed to be rivals unless there is clear, objective evidence to think of them as such.

As with other emotions, your task is to help your client to develop a flexible and non-extreme attitude towards inferred threats to her relationship with a prized other and to encourage her to act and think in ways that are consistent with her rational belief. If she feels healthily jealous rather than unhealthily jealous, she will be able to be objective about the existence of a threat to her relationship and to go along with the probability that such a threat does not exist unless she has clear evidence of its existence and come to terms with the threat if it does exist. In both cases, your client will be able to resume her coaching work towards her personal objectives. Table 7 reviews the major features of unhealthy jealousy and healthy jealousy.

Problematic envy and constructive envy

When your client has an emotional problem where unhealthy envy predominate then the adversity that features at 'A' in the 'ABC' framework will be another person having something (e.g. an object or relationship) that your client prizes,

Table 7 Unhealthy jealousy and healthy jealousy

Adversity at 'A'	Belief at 'B'	Emotion at 'C'	Behaviour at 'C'	Subsequent thinking at 'C'
Threat to your relationship with your partner from another person	Irrational	Unhealthy jealousy	• You seek constant reassurance that you are loved • You monitor the actions and feelings of your partner • You search for evidence that your partner is involved with someone else • You attempt to restrict the movements or activities of your partner • You set tests that your partner has to pass • You retaliate for your partner's presumed infidelity • You sulk	• You tend to see threats to your relationship when none really exist • You think the loss of your relationship is imminent • You misconstrue your partner's ordinary conversations with relevant others as having romantic or sexual connotations • You construct visual images of your partner's infidelity • If your partner admits to finding another person attractive, you think that s/he finds that person more attractive than you and that s/he will leave you for this other person
Threat to your relationship with your partner from another person	Rational	Healthy jealousy	• You allow your partner to express love for you without seeking reassurance • You allow your partner freedom without monitoring his/her feelings, actions and whereabouts • You allow your partner to show natural interest in members of the opposite sex without setting tests	• You tend not to see threats to your relationship when none exist • You do not misconstrue ordinary conversations between your partner and other men/women • You do not construct visual images of your partner's infidelity • You accept that your partner will find others attractive but you do not see this as a threat

does not have, but wants. For the last time, as with the other emotions that I have discussed, a rigid belief and an extreme belief mediate between the above theme at 'A' and the emotion of unhealthy envy. In unhealthy envy, your client either 'feels' deprived (non-ego unhealthy envy) or considers herself less worthy as a result of not having what the other has (ego unhealthy envy).

Aside from the emotional part of this response when your client feels unhealthy envy, her behaviour will be dominated by a wish to make things even between herself and the other person, either by getting what the other person has at all costs, to spoil the other person's possession if she cannot get it or one like it for herself or to denigrate the possession in some way. In addition, her subsequent thinking will exaggerate the importance of the possession and be dominated by plans to get the possession, to spoil it or to denigrate it. It is important to note that the major motivation of your client's behaviour and thinking when she is unhealthily envious is to make things equal.

Healthy envy is, from an RECBT theoretical perspective, deemed to be the healthy alternative to unhealthy envy (for the final time, the important point here is the term you and your client have agreed to use as the healthy alternative to unhealthy envy). It stems from a set of flexible and non-extreme beliefs about another person having something that your client prizes, does not have, but desires. Aside from the emotional part of this response when your client feels healthy envy, rather than unhealthy envy, she will be inclined, behaviourally, to pursue the possession, but only if she truly wants it. If she cannot get it, she will admire the possession without wanting to spoil it for the other or to denigrate it. Her subsequent thinking will be realistic and balanced in nature and locate the possession within an overall assessment of what the other person has and does not have in her life and what your client has and does not have in her life. As mentioned earlier, she will only make plans to get the possession if she really wants it and it will have enduring value for your client and if the costs of pursuing the possession are not too great.

As with other emotions, your task is to help your client

Table 8 Unhealthy envy and healthy envy

Adversity at 'A'	Belief at 'B'	Emotion at 'C'	Behaviour at 'C'	Subsequent thinking at 'C'
Another person possesses and enjoys something desirable that you do not have	Irrational	Unhealthy envy	• You disparage verbally the person who has the desired possession to others • You disparage verbally the desired possession to others • If you had the chance you would take away the desired possession from the other (either so that you will have it or so that the other is deprived of it) • If you had the chance you would spoil or destroy the desired possession so that the other person does not have it	• You tend to denigrate in your mind the value of the desired possession and/or the person who possesses it • You try to convince yourself that you are happy with your possessions (although you are not) • You think about how to acquire the desired possession regardless of its usefulness • You think about how to deprive the other person of the desired possession • You think about how to spoil or destroy the other's desired possession
Another person possesses and enjoys something desirable that you do not have	Rational	Healthy envy	• You strive to obtain the desired possession if it is truly what you want	• You honestly admit to yourself that you desire the desired possession • You do not try to convince yourself that you are happy with your possessions when you are not • You think about how to obtain the desired possession because you desire it for healthy reasons • You can allow the other person to have and enjoy the desired possession without denigrating that person or the possession

to develop a flexible and non-extreme attitude towards another person having something that your client prizes, does not have but desires, and to act and think in ways that are consistent with her rational belief. If she feels healthy envy rather than unhealthy envy, she will be able to come to terms with not having what the other has and to resume her coaching work towards her personal objectives. Table 8 reviews the major features of unhealthy envy and healthy envy.

Having discussed the major factors involved in the eight major UNEs and their HNE alternatives, I will proceed to outline and discuss a step-by-step guide that you can use when you help your client deal with an emotional problem that she is bogged down with and which is serving as an obstacle to her pursuing her more traditional coaching goals (i.e. her personal objectives) because she cannot bypass the problem on her own sufficiently to concentrate on her coaching goals.

Part 3

A step-by-step guide to dealing with your clients' emotional problems

Introduction

In this part of the guide, I will outline a step-by-step guide showing you how to deal with your client's emotional problem when it serves as an obstacle to her working towards her personal objectives. In doing so, I will illustrate my points by referring to the case of Linda that I discussed earlier in this book

I have mentioned several times so far in this book that when your client experiences a problematic emotion about an adversity, this only serves as an obstacle to her pursuing her personal objectives when she gets stuck in this unhealthy way of responding, cannot get out of it by herself and cannot bypass it sufficiently to focus on her coaching goals. As such, you should only help her to address this emotional problem when she gets stuck and cannot bypass it on her own. If she initially experiences a problematic emotion to an adversity, but can respond productively to this emotion using her own existing resources, then let her do so and do not intervene. Indeed, if you make such an intervention, you might indicate to your client that she is not capable of dealing with such obstacles on her own when she has such capability.

Let me reiterate a point that I made in the Introduction. Remember that your basic goal as a life coach is to help your client to identify, pursue and ultimately achieve her personal life objectives and not to help her with her emotional problems *per se* – that is the role of a psychotherapist or counsellor. Recall that the position that I take in this book is that you should only deal with your client's emotional problem when it serves as a specific obstacle to her pursuing her personal objectives because she has become stuck in an unhealthy way of responding to the adversity and cannot bypass the problem sufficiently on her own to concentrate on her coaching goals. If your client has many such emotional problems then you should refer her to a psychotherapist or counsellor to deal with these emotional problems sufficiently so that she can then engage in life coaching productively.

Having made this clear, let me stress that your first task

is to assess whether or not your client has experienced a problematic emotion to an adversity and has become bogged down in this emotion and cannot continue to pursue her personal objectives because she cannot bypass this emotional problem.

Step 1: determine whether or not your client has an emotional problem. If she has, determine whether or not she is stuck and whether or not she can bypass it to pursue her personal objectives

As you can see there are three parts to this step:

- determining whether or not your client has an emotional problem
- determining whether or not she is stuck
- determining whether or not she is able to pursue her personal objectives given that she is stuck with her emotional problem.

Determine whether or not your client has an emotional problem

In Part 2 of this book, I discussed the eight main problematic emotions that clients experience when faced with life's adversities. These eight problematic emotions are: anxiety, depression, shame, guilt, hurt, problematic anger, problematic jealousy and problematic envy. In presenting these problematic emotions (which I referred to as unhealthy negative emotions or UNEs), I outlined the major behaviours (i.e. both overt actions and action tendencies) and the subsequent thinking that tend to accompany them. You should use this material as a guide in assessing whether or not your client has an emotional problem.

Case study: Linda

Throughout this part of the book, I will illustrate my points by referring to the work I did with Linda who, you may recall, I was coaching because she was not feeling challenged in life. In our first two coaching sessions, I established where she needed to be challenged in life and we set a number of goals that she agreed to pursue before the next coaching session. Before I saw her next she learned that she failed to get promotion that had been promised to her by her boss. Let me show you how I helped Linda and myself determine whether or not she had a problem about this. As I do so, I will comment on my inner dialogue as a coach and connect this with how I intervened with Linda. I will do this to help you understand the reasons for my interventions with Linda. Where appropriate I will use this inner dialogue to make more general points about how to use RECBT in similar situations.

WINDY: Since we last met what have you done to pursue your wish to get more challenge into your life?

LINDA: Well, I felt really inspired at the end of the last session. However, a few days later I found out from my boss that he was not going to promote me even though he had promised that he would do so.

WINDY: And how do you feel about this?

LINDA: Well, I felt and still feel really upset about it.

[Windy's observation: The term 'upset' is too vague for me to determine what type of emotion Linda is feeling and whether her emotional response is unhealthy or healthy. So I need to clarify this. I will do this by using her term 'upset' but linking it with more specific negative emotions.]

WINDY: Do you feel hurt upset, angry upset or . . .?

LINDA: Angry upset definitely.

[Windy's observation: OK, so now I know that Linda is angry, but I now need to find out whether this anger is healthy or not. I will start by looking at her behaviour.]

WINDY: When you feel angry how do you express it?

LINDA: I don't.

[Windy's observation: Having drawn a blank here, I will now assess her action tendency; which is how she feels like expressing her anger but doesn't act on this feeling.]

WINDY: When you feel angry what do you feel like doing, but suppress?

LINDA: I feel like ripping him to shreds and giving him a real piece of my mind.

[Windy's observation: This seems very much like problematic or unhealthy anger, but I will double check by assessing her associated thinking.]

WINDY: And how much do you think about this?

LINDA: It keeps going round and round in my mind. I can't seem to concentrate on anything else. So although I was planning to do a lot of preparatory work for this session, I just haven't had the mental space to do any.

[Windy's observation: Since angry rumination is a feature of unhealthy anger this seems to confirm my hunch that Linda's anger is problematic for her. I will now ask her directly about this.]

WINDY: It's understandable that you feel angry about this, but anger can be healthy or unhealthy. While you don't express how you feel directly, you say that you feel like giving your boss a piece of your mind and ripping him to shreds. You also say that you are ruminating about this event a lot. Standing back for a moment, do you think that your anger is healthy or unhealthy?

LINDA: Put like that, I think it's really unhealthy.

Determine whether or not your client is stuck

As I mentioned earlier, the fact that your client has an emotional problem about an adversity does not justify you helping her with it within a life coaching context. Many people experience emotional problems that temporarily derail them, but they are able to get to grips with them and move on and this may well be the case with your client. It is only when your client gets stuck or bogged down with the emotional problem and cannot move on in the pursuit of her personal objectives either by herself or with help from others that she requires intervention from you. But how do you determine whether or not this is the case? Here are some suggestions. If your client has an emotional problem that has served as an obstacle to pursuing her personal objectives, help her with this:

1 if there has been no change in her feelings despite extended attempts at self-help
2 if there has been no change in her feelings despite extended attempts at seeking informal help from others
3 if she has no plans to deal with this emotional problem in the future and it is likely to continue
4 if she cannot bypass this problem to refocus on her coaching goals (see next section).

Case study: Linda

> *WINDY:* What have you tried to do to help yourself deal with your anger?
>
> *LINDA:* Well, I have discussed what happened with my partner and friends, but they just seem to think that my anger is justified. My partner wants to confront my boss and 'punch his lights out'. I have tried punching a cushion and doing relaxation exercises, but nothing seems to help apart from in the very short term.
>
> *[Windy's observation: It seems that nothing Linda has tried has helped her to deal with her problematic anger. Let's see if she has any plans to deal with it more effectively.]*
>
> *WINDY:* Do you have any plans to deal with your anger?
>
> *LINDA:* I was hoping that you might be able to help me in this respect.
>
> *[Windy's observation: Sounds like a specific invitation for me to intervene. But first, I want to double check to see if Linda's anger is an obstacle to her pursuing her personal objectives.]*

Determine whether or not being stuck with the emotional problem prevents your client from pursuing her personal objectives

Although your client may be bogged down with her emotional problem, it does not follow that this will necessarily prevent her from pursuing the personal objectives that she set with you earlier in the coaching process. Having said that, if she is stuck, then it is unlikely that she will have the mental space to detach from the problem and pursue her objectives. However, please note that I said 'unlikely' here and not 'impossible'. Some people are able to compartmentalize and pursue objectives in one area of their lives, while being emotionally bogged down in another area. So, even if you have a strong suspicion that your client will not be able to pursue her personal objectives because she is stuck in dealing with her emotional problem, it is still important that you check this out with her in case you are wrong.

Case study: Linda

> *WINDY:* You said earlier that after our last session you felt inspired to put into practice what we discussed. Then, a few days later you found out that you were not going to get the promotion you were promised. Now, we have established that you feel unhealthily angry about this and we know that you feel stuck with your angry feelings. Is that right?
>
> *LINDA:* That's correct.
>
> *[Windy's observation: Now I need to establish whether or not Linda is able to compartmentalize this problem and keep working towards her personal objectives.]*
>
> *WINDY:* Have you been able to 'park' your angry feelings and keep working towards your personal objectives or have they gotten in the way of you doing so?

> *LINDA:* To be honest with you, I have let our work go because my mind has been on the promotion issue.
>
> *[Windy's observation: Finally, I'm going to assess whether or not Linda will be able to compartmentalize her angry feelings in the future.]*
>
> *WINDY:* And do you think that on your own you will be able to 'park' these feelings in the future and concentrate on our work together or do you think you might want some help to deal with your unhealthy feelings?
>
> *LINDA:* I don't think that I would know how to 'park' these feelings as you call it. I would value some help.

Your client is stuck, but can compartmentalize and can work towards her personal objectives: three ways forward

Now, what if your client can compartmentalize her emotional problem despite being stuck, and can keep working towards her personal objectives? In such a case, you have three ways forward.

1 *You can keep helping your client to work towards her personal objectives without helping her to deal with her emotional problem.*

In this case, you leave her to decide if and how she wants to tackle her emotional problem.

2 *You can keep helping her to work towards her objectives and offer to help her get unstuck with respect to the emotional problem.*

In this case, recognize that you are moving into a counselling role with your client and thus, your coaching contract with her may need to be renegotiated accordingly. You are moving into a counselling role here because you are departing from your coaching brief – which is to help your client reach her personal objectives – when it is not necessary for you to do so, since she is still able to work towards her personal objectives despite being stuck with her emotional problem. In my view, you are remaining in a coaching role when the presence of your client's emotional problem does prevent her from working towards her personal objectives since your goal here is to help her get unstuck so that she can resume her pursuit of her goals.

3   *You could keep helping her work towards her objectives and refer her to a counsellor who will help her with her emotional problem.*

Whichever of these three options you choose will depend on (1) how you construe your role as a coach, and (2) the views of your client.

Please note that some coaches choose not to take on a counselling role and will therefore not take Option 2 above, while others are happy to move from coaching to counselling and back again. In my experience, those in the latter group tend to be coaches who have previously trained as counsellors.

It is also important to note in this context that some clients may have deliberately sought coaching even if they need counselling in some area of their lives. With such clients, the very mention of counselling may put them off and spoil the working alliance that you have with them as a coach.

Case study: Linda

Having established that Linda had an emotional problem, was bogged down with it and could not compartmentalize it, I discussed with her how we might deal with this.

> WINDY: OK, now there are a couple of possibilities here. First, I could help you with this emotional problem myself. This would involve me temporarily assuming a counselling role. Because it is temporary, doing so is not incompatible with my work as a coach. Second, I could refer you to a

> counselling colleague who will help you with
> this and when you are ready, we could resume
> our coaching work. What's your view?
> *LINDA:* Well, if you can help me with this I would like
> you to help me with the problem.

It is important to stress that any movement from coaching to counselling needs to be carefully explored with your client and explicitly agreed with her. This is definitely an issue that you should discuss with your coaching supervisor.

My final advice on this issue is for you to avoid switching from coaching to counselling with clients who have particular difficulties handling situations where roles are ambiguous.

In proceeding with this book, let me stress that I shall be dealing with situations where a client is:

- working with you in coaching, has specified and is pursuing a set of personal objectives
- has encountered an emotional problem that is interfering with her pursuing her personal objectives
- has agreed to work with you to deal with this emotional problem so that she can resume the pursuit of her coaching goals.

Step 2: elicit your client's explicit agreement to target this emotional problem for change and establish a contingency plan if you fail to help her

Developing a good working alliance between you and your client is an important ingredient of effective coaching (Bordin, 1979; Dryden, 2006). Such an alliance depends on (1) having a good bond between the two of you, (2) having a shared view of the coaching process, (3) agreeing on your client's personal objectives goals, and (4) agreeing on what you and your client are going to do to help her achieve her objectives.

At this point in the coaching process you are deviating from your main role as a coach – which is to help your client to achieve her personal objectives. Instead, you are adopting a temporary role of helping your client to remove the emotional obstacle that is preventing her from doing her work to achieve her personal objectives. You may think, at this point, that you and your client have agreed to target for change her emotional problem, which is serving as an obstacle to her working towards her goal, but it is important that you explicitly do so. Some coaches prefer to document this agreement in writing. Whether or not you choose this more formal approach, my advice is to err on the side of caution and to reiterate this agreement and make it explicit. This is best done in a summary statement of what you and your client have discussed so far concerning the emotional obstacle to the pursuit of her personal objectives.

In addition, you need to consider what you and your client are going to do if your attempts to help her with her emotional problems are not successful. Making a contingency plan for this eventuality at this stage is good ethical practice. What are your options here? You can do either of the following.

1 Renegotiate your contract with your client from a coaching contract to a counselling contract. Effectively this means that you will help her with this problem more intensively and with any other emotional problems that

she may have and refer her to another coach when she is ready to resume her pursuit of her personal objectives.

2 Refer her to a counsellor who will work with her on this emotional problem until she is ready to resume her coaching work with you.

Case study: Linda

WINDY: So, Linda, let me summarize where we have got to so far. OK?

LINDA: OK.

WINDY: In our coaching work, we had identified your wish to be challenged more in life and you had been quite excited about beginning to identify how you might go about seeking such challenges. Then, your boss, who had promised to promote you, didn't do so. You responded with anger and we established that this anger is problematic in the sense that you have become stuck in your angry feelings and can't 'park' it sufficiently to keep focused on your coaching objective. Is this accurate?

LINDA: Very.

WINDY: We further considered how we were going to deal with this obstacle and we agreed that I was going to help you deal with this obstacle myself. Is that your understanding?

LINDA: Yes it is.

WINDY: OK. Before we start, let's consider what happens if I can't help you with this obstacle. OK?

LINDA: OK.

WINDY: We need to establish a contingency plan to deal with this situation. I suggest that if this happens that I refer you to one of my colleagues who is a counsellor and who would work with you more intensively to deal with this emotional problem. Then, when you are ready, we would resume our coaching work. How does that sound?

LINDA: Sounds good.

WINDY: OK, so let's go forward on that basis. OK?

LINDA: OK.

Step 3: formulate the problem that is serving as an obstacle to the pursuit of your client's personal objectives

When you focus on an emotional obstacle to the pursuit of your client's personal objectives in the context of coaching, you will only be dealing with a single specific problem. Otherwise, you will be involved in counselling, not coaching

You will have already established that your client has an emotional problem in Step 1. It is useful to summarize what you already know before proceeding.

Case study: Linda

> WINDY: Now we are focusing on your emotional problem, let me just review what you told me when we first talked about it. OK?
>
> LINDA: OK.
>
> WINDY: You made yourself angry about your boss not promoting you after telling you that he would. We discovered that your anger was unhealthy because you felt like ripping him to shreds and you were ruminating about the situation. Is that correct?
>
> LINDA: Yes, it is.

Formulate your client's emotional problem using the 'situational ABC' framework

When you help your client to formulate her emotional problem, you have a clear statement of this problem informed by the 'situational ABC' framework that I discussed earlier in the book.

I suggest that you use the following points in formulating your client's emotional problem.

1 **[Situation]** – Help your client to identify the situation in which she experiences her problem.

2 **['A']** – 'A' is the aspect of the situation that your client was most disturbed about. It is not necessary to identify 'A' at this point since you will do so in Step 8.

3 **['C' (emotional)]** – Help your client to identify the *one* major UNE that she experiences in the situation specified above. This will be one of the following: anxiety, depression, guilt, shame, hurt, problematic anger, problematic jealousy and problematic envy.

4 **['C' (behavioural)]** – Help your client to identify the dysfunctional behaviour that your client demonstrated in this situation. Remember this might be an overt action or an action tendency.

5 **['C' (cognitive)]** – If relevant, help your client to identify the thinking your client engaged in once her UNE 'kicked in'.

6 **[Effect on coaching goals]** – Help your client to specify the effect that this emotional problem has on your client's coaching goals.

Case study: Linda

Let me use my work with Linda and show how the above framework can be used.

1 Situation: *My boss told me that I would get promotion, but then he did not promote me.*

2 'A': *Not known yet.*

3 'C' (emotional): *Unhealthy anger.*

4 'C' (behavioural): *Felt like ripping my boss to shreds.*

5 'C' (cognitive): *Ruminating about not being promoted and what I would like to do to my boss.*

6 Effect on coaching goals: *This is stopping me from concentrating on and pursuing my coaching goals.*

Putting this into a sentence we have Linda's formulated problem.

My boss told me that I would get promotion, but then he did not promote me. I feel unhealthily angry about this and feel like ripping my boss to shreds. I ruminate about doing so and about not being promoted. This is stopping me from concentrating on and pursuing my coaching goals.

Step 4: set a goal with respect to the formulated problem

It is useful at this point to help your client to set a goal with respect to her formulated target problem. Doing so gives your work on her emotional problem a sense of direction and helps your client to see that change is possible, which engenders a sense of hope and increases her motivation to engage in the process of RECBT.

Set your client's goal with respect to her formulated problem using the 'situational ABC' framework

I suggest that you use the following points in helping your client to set a goal with respect to her formulated target emotional problem.

1 **[Situation]** – Help your client to identify the situation in which your client experiences her problem. This will be the same as she specified in her formulated target problem.

2 **['A']** – Help your client to identify the theme of the problem. This will again be the same as your client specified in her formulated target problem. However, as mentioned above, it is not necessary for you to have done this since you will do it in Step 8.

3 **['C' (emotional goal)]** – Help your client to identify the healthy alternative to the major UNE that she experienced. Note that this emotional goal should be negative because it is about an adversity, but it should also be healthy in the sense that it will enable your client to deal effectively with the adversity if it can be changed or to adjust constructively to it if it cannot be changed. This will be one of the following: concern (as opposed to anxiety), sadness (as opposed to depression), remorse (as opposed to guilt), disappointment (as opposed to shame), sorrow (as opposed to hurt), non-problematic anger (as opposed to problematic anger), non-problematic jealousy (as opposed to problematic jealousy) and non-problematic envy (as opposed to problematic envy). It is important

that you use your client's language when selecting an emotional goal and not necessarily the relevant term suggested by REBT theory (Dryden, 1986).

4 **['C' (behavioural goal)]** – Help your client to identify the functional alternative to the unconstructive behaviour that she demonstrated in her formulated target problem. Again this might be an overt action or an action tendency.

5 **['C' (cognitive goal)]** – If relevant, help your client to identify the realistic alternative to the distorted thinking that she engaged in.

Note that when you help your client to set a goal for her formulated target problem, she is only changing her emotional, behavioural and thinking responses to the situation that she finds problematic. If she feels, acts and thinks in a healthy way in response to this situation she is more likely to change the situation if it can be changed or adjust constructively and move on if it cannot be changed. Having a healthy set of responses will also help your client to refocus on and pursue her personal objectives that you originally helped her to set in coaching.

Let me show how I used the above framework to help Linda set goals with respect to her emotional problem.

Case study: Linda

WINDY: OK, Linda, let's see how you would like to handle the situation of being passed over for promotion by your boss. OK?

LINDA: OK.

WINDY: Well, we know that this situation happened so we can't do anything to prevent it from happening. Right?

LINDA: Well, I hope to get him to change his mind.

WINDY: Indeed, but you can't undo the past can you?

LINDA: Sadly no.

WINDY: You mentioned you hope to get your boss to change his mind. Will your unhealthy anger and suppressing your wish to tear him to shreds help you to do this?

[Windy's observation: Here I am preparing the ground for setting goals by encouraging Linda to see the link between her unhealthy anger and her preferred outcome.]

LINDA: No, it won't.
WINDY: So would you be interested in a way of responding that reflects the negativity of your boss not keeping his promise to promote you, but enables you to assert yourself with him and also to resume your work towards your coaching goals without being preoccupied with the situation?

[Windy's observation: Here, I am suggesting that Linda considers a goal comprising what in RECBT we call a healthy negative emotion (HNE) and related behavioural and cognitive responses.]

LINDA: That sounds good.
WINDY: So I could help you feel healthily angry rather than unhealthily angry about your boss not promoting you. This would lead you to be assertive with him rather than wanting to rip him to shreds. Also, it would help you to get on with things with this in the back of your mind rather than ruminating on it. How does that sound?

[Windy's observation: In this intervention, I am explicitly contrasting unhealthy anger with healthy anger and their respective behavioural and cognitive responses.]

LINDA: Well, if you can help me do that, it would be great.

Here, more formally, are the goals set by Linda whose emotional problem was formulated in Step 3. As noted above, the first two points are the same in the goal section as in the formulated problem section.

1 Situation: *My boss told me that I would get promotion, but then he did not promote me.*
2 'A': *Not known yet.*
3 'C' (emotional goal): *Healthy anger (rather than unhealthy anger).*
4 'C' (behavioural): *Telling my boss that I was annoyed about this and asking him to explain his decision (rather than wanting to rip him to shreds).*
5 'C' (cognitive): *Being aware of his decision, but getting on with things (rather than ruminating about it).*
6 Effect on coaching goals: *Being able to concentrate on and pursue my coaching goals.*

Putting this into a sentence we have the client's goal with respect to her formulated target problem:

My boss told me that I would get promotion, but then he did not promote me. I want to feel healthy anger (rather than unhealthy anger) about this and to tell him that I was annoyed about this and then ask him to explain his decision (rather than wanting to rip him to shreds). I want to be aware of his decision, but get on with things (rather than ruminating about it). Doing this will help me to concentrate on and pursue my coaching goals.

Note that under the headings of 'emotional goal', 'behavioural goal' and 'cognitive goal', I suggest that you encourage your client to use 'rather than' wording to highlight the difference between her problem response and her goal response. However, if she finds doing this cumbersome, then suggest she omits the 'rather than' phrases.

Step 5: assess for the presence of a meta-emotional problem and decide with the client if this is to become the target problem

When your client has an emotional problem she may focus on this problem and disturb herself about it. Given this, it is important that you assess for the existence of what in RECBT is called her meta-emotional problem (literally an emotional problem about an emotional problem or a behavioural problem)

Thus, I suggest that you ask your client a question such as:

How do you feel about . . . (state your client's original emotional/behavioural problem)?

If your client does have a meta-emotional problem you both need to decide if you need to deal with this before you both focus on her original problem.

My advice is that you suggest to your client that you both focus on her original emotional/behavioural problem unless:

• the client wants to work on her meta-emotional problem first
• the existence of the client's meta-emotional problem will interfere with her focusing on her original emotional/behavioural problem in the session
• the existence of the client's meta-emotional problem will interfere with her working on her original emotional/behavioural problem in her life.

The important point is that you and your client agree on which of her problems (the original or her meta-emotional problem) to work on first. If you target her original problem and help her with this effectively, you may not need to help her with her meta-emotional problem if your client can resume work on her coaching goal without doing so.

Case study: Linda

Here is how I addressed this issue with Linda.

WINDY: OK. So you can see that your anger is unhealthy. Can you also see that healthy anger, where you feel like asserting yourself and in fact do assert yourself with your boss, and where you get on with life, mindful of the incident, but without rumination, is constructive.

LINDA: Yes.

WINDY: Before we get down to the business of helping you, I just want to bring up one issue. Now, when you make yourself unhealthily angry and you focus on that anger how do you feel about your angry feelings?

LINDA: Well . . . I'm not sure what you mean.

WINDY: OK. For example, do you feel ashamed of feeling that way, or anxious . . .?

LINDA: Oh, I see. No. I am too busy feeling angry . . .

WINDY: What about when you calm down and focus on your anger then?

[Windy's observation: This is an important point. Your clients may disturb themselves about their UNE either at the time or later when they are not in the grip of such feelings. It is worth asking about both possibilities.]

LINDA: No, if anything I feel justified in how I feel . . . But, now I can see that there is the possibility of feeling and reacting with healthy anger, I guess I can feel justified in feeling anger and still be healthy.

[Windy's observation: Linda raises a number of important points here. First, your client may well construe their UNE positively and this needs to be tackled if it persists later in the process. Second, your client may change her mind about the perceived benefit of her UNE when she

understands and commits herself to the healthy alterna-
tive to this UNE (i.e. her HNE).]

WINDY: Good point. So as you don't have what we call a
meta-emotional problem, literally an emo-
tional problem about your unhealthy anger,
we can proceed to helping you deal with your
unhealthy anger.

Step 6: ask for a concrete example of the client's formulated target problem

Once you have helped your client to formulate her problem and set a related goal. I suggest that you help her to select a concrete example of this problem. Working with a concrete example will provide you both with specific information about your client's 'A' and 'C', which will help you to identify a specific irrational belief at 'B'. If your client's problem is specific enough anyway, then you may skip this step. If not, ask your client:

> Can you give me a concrete example of this problem?

A concrete example is one that occurred in a specific situation at a specific time in the presence of a specific person or persons.

If your client finds it difficult to select a concrete example of her target problem, you can suggest that she pick an example that is fresh in her mind. This example might be:

- recent
- vivid
- typical
- future.

It may seem strange to talk about a future example of the client's problem, but if you think about it, it is not so strange. Your client may imagine a future scenario and when she does so, she may disturb herself about it because she brings to that future event a disturbance creating irrational belief. In what follows, Linda selects a future example of her emotional problem and you will see how I handled this.

Case study: Linda

WINDY: So now let's discuss your unhealthy anger. It would be useful if you could pick a specific example of your anger problem with your boss. This might be something that has happened, is happening or you anticipate happening.

LINDA: Well, I would like to talk to him about it, but I think if I do I will lose my temper.

WINDY: So, let's focus on that. Can you tell me about the specific situation you envisage?

[Windy's observation: As Linda has chosen a future specific example, I need to get as much detail as I can about this likely context.]

LINDA: Well, it would be in his office just before lunch and I would have asked to see him about not being promoted.

[Windy's observation: This is sufficient detail to go on to the next step.]

Step 7: identify 'C'

At this point you may well know the specific feeling that your client experienced in the specific example that she has selected for assessment. After all, you will have formulated her emotional problem and the relevant UNE should have been made explicit in this formulation. However, there may be times when the UNE has not been specified in this formulation and it is only when your client discusses a specific example of her emotional problem that the relevant UNE becomes clear.

As you will remember, 'C' stands for the consequences of your client's irrational beliefs about 'A'. 'C' can be emotional, behavioural and cognitive. It is important at this point that you assess your client's major UNE in the selected example. If she experiences several, help her to select the main one. Additionally, if you can also identify the associated behaviour that would be good. Identifying the subsequent thinking is, in my opinion, optional if you have assessed the emotional and behavioural aspects of 'C'

However, why begin with 'C'? Why not start with 'A'? In my view, if you start with 'C' and, in particular, your client's major UNE, this emotion helps you to identify her 'A' by giving you clues concerning the likely theme of the 'A'. For example, if your client says that she feels anxious, you know that the theme of 'threat' is likely to be present in her 'A'. I refer you to the material I outlined in Part 2 of this book where I discussed the main cognitive behavioural features of the eight UNEs and their HNE alternatives. As I said earlier, 'C' can be behavioural, cognitive as well as emotional, but I suggest that you start with the emotional 'C' since this is the component that will most aid you in then assessing your client's 'C'.

Start with the emotional 'C'

Ask the client to identify how she felt in the situation in question. Help her to select one UNE and, if she felt several, help her to identify the main one. Thus, you can ask:

> How did you feel when . . . (state the situation) . . .?

When all goes well, your client will clearly state that her emotional 'C' is both negative and unhealthy. However, the course of RECBT, like the course of true love, rarely runs smoothly and if you encounter the following here is what I suggest you do.

Your client's emotional 'C' is vague

Here, your client may say that she 'feels' bad or upset. Such expressions of negative emotion are unclear and when stated thus, you do not know what your client's negative emotional 'C' is, nor do you know if it is unhealthy or healthy. When this happens it is important that you help your client to be more specific about her feelings.

For example:

> COACH: How did you feel when your dad quickly passed
>   you on to your mum when you phoned home?
> CLIENT: I felt bad.
> COACH: I am not sure what emotion that refers to. Can
>   you be more specific?
> CLIENT: I felt hurt.

You are not sure if your client's negative 'C' is healthy or unhealthy

While REBT theory is clear in its language when differentiating between UNEs and HNEs (see Tables 1–8) your client is unlikely to use the same language when referring to her emotions. Thus, your client may give you an emotion that sounds like a UNE, but you are not sure whether it is or not. Alternatively, in response to your request to be specific about her negative emotion, your client may continue to be vague about her feelings.

What can you do in such circumstances? If you look at the Tables 1–8, you will see that apart from the different names given to unhealthy and negative emotion pairs, each emotion within a pairing (e.g. anxiety and concern) is associated with different behaviours (i.e. overt actions and action tendencies) and subsequent thinking. Given this, it is possible to infer your client's emotion by discovering how she acted in the situation that you are assessing and/or how she thought after her feelings had 'kicked in'. Let me show what I mean by revisiting the example above.

COACH: How did you feel when your dad quickly passed you on to your mum when you phoned home?

CLIENT: I felt bad.

COACH: I am not sure what emotion that refers to. Can you be more specific?

CLIENT: I am not sure that I can.

COACH: OK. When you felt bad about your dad quickly passing you on to your mum when you phoned, what did you do or feel like doing?

CLIENT: I felt like putting the phone down.

COACH: Why?

CLIENT: Because I felt that my dad always does this to me and wouldn't do that if it was my sister who rang.

COACH: Could you tell your dad how you feel at that point?

CLIENT: No.

COACH: Why not?

CLIENT: Because I don't feel like talking to him when he does that. I just want to go into my shell and make him suffer.

COACH: So, correct me if I am wrong, but my sense is that you felt hurt when your father quickly passed the phone on to your mother? Is that right?

CLIENT: Very much so. I did feel hurt.

By utilizing the information provided in Tables 1–8 and matching it to what his client said about how she felt like acting (i.e. her action tendency) and how she thought in the situation when she felt 'bad', the coach hypothesized that his client's 'C' was hurt, a hunch that was confirmed by his client.

Your client's stated emotional 'C' is really an inference

As I discussed earlier in the book, when your client's emotional problem serves as an impediment to the coaching work that you are doing together in the service of her personal objectives, she is likely to experience a major UNE such as: anxiety, depression, guilt, shame, hurt, unhealthy anger, unhealthy jealousy, unhealthy envy. She may experience more than one such emotion and if so, you need to deal with one emotion at a time.

Having said this, when you ask your client what emotion she experienced in the specific example of her emotional problem, she may not give you one of the above listed emotions. Apart from being vague about her feelings (which I discussed on p. 76), your client may say that her emotion is really an inference when you ask her for her emotional 'C'. As we saw earlier, an inference is an interpretation that your client made about the situation that she was in that was related to her emotional response but which went beyond the data at hand. Your client may have been correct in making her inference or she may have been incorrect. However, she may think that her inference was factual. Actually, these 'inferences as emotions' frequently turn out to be your client's 'A's'.

Here are some examples of inferences that clients mistake for emotions:

- 'I felt rejected'
- 'I felt criticized'
- 'I felt attacked'
- 'I felt wronged'.

As you can see none of the above represent a client's emotional 'C'. They are inferences. For example, when your client says that she 'felt wronged', she means that the person in the specific example of her emotional problem that she has chosen, acted in a way that transgressed one of your client's rules. It is highly probable that your client experienced an emotion about 'being wronged' and, if you have done your work well up to this point, it is likely that this emotion is a UNE (i.e. negative and unhealthy). But what is important to note is that your client has not been explicit about this emotional 'C'. It is your job to help your client to do this. Here are some examples of how to do so.

THE 'ABOUT' METHOD

Here is what you do when you use the 'about' method. When your client provides you with an inference instead of an emotion in response to your enquiry about her emotional 'C', you treat her response as an inference and ask the client how she felt *about* this inference.

> *COACH:* How did you feel when your boss gave you feedback about your report?
> *CLIENT:* I felt criticized.
> *COACH:* Do you mean that your boss was criticizing you or just your report?
>
> *[Windy's observation: Here the coach seeks to clarify whether the criticism referred to criticism of her work or criticism of her entire self. The latter proved to be the case.]*
>
> *CLIENT:* I thought he was criticizing me as a person.
> *COACH:* And when you thought that your boss was criticizing you as a person how did you feel *about* his criticism?
> *CLIENT:* I felt hurt about that.

CAUTION

When your client gives you an inference when you have asked for her emotional 'C' and this inference is clearly distorted, you may well be tempted to focus on this inference with a view to encouraging your client to question it. It is important to resist this temptation for two reasons. First, your task at this point is to help your client to identify her emotional 'C' in the specific example of her emotional problem that she has selected. If you switch to questioning her inference, then you are not going to identify this emotional 'C'. Second, when you help your client to question her inference without identifying her underlying irrational belief and helping her to question and change it, then you are not helping her as fully as you can. In RECBT we say that since your clients' emotional problems are largely determined by their irrational beliefs, rather than their distorted inferences, then the best way of helping them with emotional problems is to help them to develop a healthier set of rational belief alternatives rather than a set of realistic inferences. The problem with encouraging your client to make an inferential change rather than a belief-based change is that the relief (albeit short term) that she gets from changing her inference will lessen her motivation to change her irrational belief.

In summary, when your client gives you an inference instead of an emotion at this juncture, remember to use the inference to identify the emotional 'C' and resist the temptation to question the inference.

Ask for behavioural and/or thinking 'C's' and infer the emotional 'C'

If for any reason your client continues to struggle to give you an emotional 'C', then you can temporarily bypass this and infer the emotion from her behaviour (overt action and action tendency) or her subsequent thinking. Before doing so, I suggest that you familiarize yourself with Tables 1–8 in Part 2 of this book.

What you do is this:

- ask your client to imagine that she is in the situation that she selected in which she experienced her emotional problem
- assess how she acted in this situation or what she felt like doing, but did not do so

- if necessary, ask her what thoughts she had after her 'yet to be identified' feelings had 'kicked in'
- form a hypothesis concerning what your client's emotional 'C' could have been given her behavioural 'C' and/or thinking 'C'
- ask your client to consider this.

Here is an example of this approach in practice.

COACH: So how did you feel when you discovered that your friend had divulged your confidence to another mutual friend?

CLIENT: I felt bad about it.

COACH: Can you clarify that emotion a bit more?

CLIENT: I am not sure that I can.

COACH: OK, is it alright if I ask you a number of specific questions that will help both of us discover the nature of your emotion?

CLIENT: OK.

COACH: Great. Cast your mind back to when you first discovered that your friend had divulged your confidence to another common friend. What did you do?

CLIENT: Well I bitched about it to my friends.

[Windy's observation: This doesn't really help the coach. He needs to focus his client's attention on how she behaved to her friend or on what she felt like doing, but did not actually do.]

COACH: OK what did you do to your friend who betrayed your trust in this way?

CLIENT: I didn't do anything.

COACH: Did you feel an urge to say or do something to your friend that in the end you suppressed?

CLIENT: Funny you should ask that, because I did have to suppress an urge to do something to her.

COACH: And what was that urge?

> *CLIENT:*   Well, I wanted to sulk and not talk to her and to spread some nasty gossip about her.
>
> *[Windy's observation: The client is giving clues that she either felt angry about her friend's behaviour or hurt about it.]*
>
> *COACH:*   So by the sound of it you felt either unhealthy anger or hurt.
>
> *CLIENT:*   Well, I think it was both of those feelings. I mainly felt hurt though and my anger was secondary to that.

So, in this example, the client revealed in response to the coach's specific line of questioning that she felt both hurt and unhealthy anger, but that her hurt was her main UNE.

Case study: Linda

You will recall that when I asked Linda for a specific example of her anger problem she chose a future example where she would be in her boss's office just before lunch having asked to see him about not being promoted. This is how I identified her emotional 'C' in this situation.

> *WINDY:*   So how do you think you will feel in your boss's office just before lunch having asked to see him about not being promoted?
>
> *LINDA:*   I would feel angry.
>
> *[Windy's observation: Although Linda's formulated problem is unhealthy anger, I am not going to assume that her anger in the specific example she has chosen is necessarily unhealthy. I need to get evidence before concluding that it is and helping Linda to see this.]*
>
> *WINDY:*   Your anger could be healthy or unhealthy and I would like to clarify which it is if that is OK?

LINDA: That's fine.

WINDY: When you anticipate feeling angry what would you feel like doing at that moment?

LINDA: I wouldn't do this, of course, but I would feel like shouting abuse at him and giving him a slap.

WINDY: Now does that sound like healthy anger to you?

LINDA (laughing): Certainly not!

Step 8: identify 'A'

Remember that 'A' is the inference the client makes about the situation that triggers 'B'

While you are assessing 'A', it is important for you to remember that 'A' is the most relevant part of the situation that triggered your client's irrational belief at 'B', which, in turn, largely determined her UNE at 'C'.

The standard question in assessing 'A'

When you assess 'A', here is the most common way of doing so. Ask:

> What were you most ... about (state the client's 'C') when ... (state the situation)?

If I was using this question with Linda, I would ask:

> What do you think you will be most unhealthily angry about when you see your boss in his office to talk about why you were not promoted?

Windy's magic question

Here is another method, which I call 'Windy's magic question' if the above question does not yield the 'A'.

1 Focus on the 'situation' that your client has described.
2 Ask her what one thing would get rid of or significantly diminish the UNE that she felt at 'C'.
3 The opposite to this is your client's 'A'.

Case study: Linda

Here is how I would have used this method with Linda.

Her described 'situation' is: 'Going to see my boss in his office at lunchtime to talk about me not being promoted' and her emotional 'C' was unhealthy anger.

1 Focus your client's attention on the 'situation' that she described: *'Going to see my boss in his office at lunchtime to talk about me not being promoted'*.
2 Ask her what one thing would get rid of or significantly diminish the anxiety that she felt at 'C': *'That my boss had not broken his promise to me'*.
3 The opposite of this is your client's 'A': *'My boss broke his promise to me'*.

Encourage your client to assume temporarily that 'A' is true

When you assess 'A', you may discover that your client's 'A' is a clear distortion of reality. If this is the case, you may be tempted to question 'A'. As I discussed in the previous step, it is important that you resist this temptation. Rather, at this stage you should encourage your client to assume temporarily that 'A' is correct. For example, in the case previously described, it is not important to determine whether your client's boss has broken his promise to her. What is important is that you encourage your client to assume that 'A' is correct in order to help her to identify more accurately the irrational beliefs about the 'A' that led to her feelings at 'C'. Later, you will have an opportunity to check whether 'A' is likely to have been true (see Step 21, pp. 161–164).

There may be times when your client will want to question 'A' and not want to go on to identify her irrational beliefs at 'B'. I suggest that you go along with this, but only after you have made several attempts to show her the importance of identifying irrational beliefs. If these fail, not questioning 'A' at this point would threaten the working alliance you have with your client. If you need to question 'A' at this point proceed straight to Step 21.

Avoid pitfalls in assessing 'A'

There are a number of pitfalls in assessing 'A'. The following suggestions can help you to avoid them.

1 Do not obtain too much detail about the situation in which the client's 'A' is embedded. Allowing your client to talk at length about the situation can discourage you both from retaining a problem-solving approach to overcoming her emotional problems. If your client does provide too much detail, try to abstract the salient theme or summarize what you understand to be her 'A'. Interrupt your client tactfully and re-establish an RECBT-driven assessment focus if she does begin to discuss the situation at length. For example, you could say, 'I think you may be giving me more detail than I require. What was it about the situation that you were most disturbed about?'

2 Do not assume that the first inference that your client comes up with is her 'A'. Ask for other inferences that she might have made in the situation, then apply 'Windy's magic question' (see above) to identify your client's 'A'.

3 Do not accept an 'A' unless it reflects the theme associated with the UNE you have already assessed. Consult Tables 1–8 for information about inferential themes associated with the eight emotional problems for which clients typically seek help.

Identify 'A': Linda

Here is how I identified Linda's 'A'.

> WINDY: So what do you think you will be most angry about when you go to see your boss to discuss not being promoted?
>
> LINDA: Well, he said he would promote me and then he didn't do so.
>
> WINDY: So apart from giving you promotion, what could you discover at the meeting that would

> eliminate or significantly reduce your unhealthy anger?

[Windy's observation: This is a version of 'Windy's magic question' technique explained above.]

LINDA: Well, I am pretty sure that he will try to wriggle out of it, but I think that if he convinced me that he hadn't broken his promise to me, then that would definitely help.

WINDY: So would I be correct in assuming, then, that you would be most unhealthily angry about your boss breaking his promise to you and not promoting you when he said he would?

LINDA: Absolutely. I really do have a thing about broken promises.

Step 9: elicit your client's emotional goal in the specific example being assessed

As a coach, it is important that your work is forward looking and this means that you will encourage your client to set personal objectives that gives the coaching work a positive direction. When dealing with your client's emotional problem obstacle to the pursuit of her personal objectives, there are two places that you will want to set goals which also give this 'overcoming obstacles' work a forward-looking thrust. I have already discussed the first place in Step 4 when I showed you how you can help your client to set a goal with respect to her formulated problem. The second place is here after you have assessed the 'A' and 'C' elements of your client's selected specific example of her formulated problem.

Thinking about your client's goal in the specific example under consideration

Before eliciting your client's goal with respect to her selected specific example, it is important to compare what you mean by this and what your client might mean by it. In RECBT, when we think about a client's goals concerning a specific example, we think in terms of the situation and the 'A' remaining constant with the client responding differently at 'C'. However, your client may have a very different idea about her goal. Let me take Linda as an example here and demonstrate what I mean. First, I will outline the 'ABC' of the specific example of Linda's problem.

Case study: Linda

Problem	Goal
Situation	*Situation*
Going to see my boss in his office at lunchtime to talk about me not being promoted	Going to see my boss in his office at lunchtime to talk about me not being promoted

'A'	*'A'*
My boss broke his promise to me	My boss broke his promise to me
'B'	*'B'*
Not yet assessed	Not yet assessed
'C'	*'C'*
Emotional C: Unhealthy anger	Emotional 'C' goal: Alternative emotion – (healthy and negative)
Behavioural 'C': Feeling like shouting abuse at him and giving him a slap	Behavioural 'C' goal: Alternative overt behaviour or action tendency – (constructive)

Now, imagine that when I asked Linda what her goal would be with respect to her response in the forthcoming meeting with her boss she said: 'To get my boss to change his mind and keep his promise to promote me'. I will call this her 'hypothetical response' in which she points to two things:

- an allusion to her behaviour although it is not clear what this behaviour is
- a change in the behaviour of her boss.

In reality, I helped Linda to set a goal that was in her power to achieve; which I will call her 'actual response' as shown below.

1 Situation: *Going to see my boss in his office at lunch-time to talk about me not being promoted.*
2 'A': *My boss broke his promise to me.*
3 'B': *Not yet assessed.*
4 'C' (emotional): *Healthy anger.*
5 'C' (behavioural): *Asserting myself to my boss and advancing cogent reasons for my promotion.*

Let me now compare her actual response with her

hypothetical response (i.e. To get my boss to change his mind and keep his promise to promote me") – see Table 9.

You will see from this table that in her hypothetical response:

- Linda did not set a clear HNE as an emotional goal. In fact she did not mention an emotional goal at all
- Linda was unclear about her behavioural goal
- Linda set as a goal a change in another person.

You will further see from Table 9 that in her actual response:

- Linda did set a clear HNE as an emotional goal
- Linda was clear about her behavioural goal
- Linda did not set as a goal a change in another person.

Summary of dos and don'ts

In summary, when eliciting your client's goal with respect to her response to the situation in which her emotional problem occurred or is likely to occur, you should ideally follow these dos and don'ts:

- do help your client to specify a HNE in response to the situation in which the adversity at 'A' occurred (or is likely to occur)
- do help your client to specify a constructive behavioural response to this 'A'
- don't help your client to set goals that are outside her direct control (e.g. a change in the behaviour of another person).

Table 9 Linda's actual and hypothetical responses when asked for a goal concerning her selected specific example. HNE, healthy negative emotion

	Actual response	Hypothetical response
Clear HNE specified	Yes	No
Specific constructive behaviour specified	Yes	No
Change in another person specified	No	Yes

Help your client to understand that changing her emotional 'C' will increase her chances of bringing about a change in 'A' if it can be changed

When you attempt to elicit a goal from your client with respect to her selected specific example of her target problem, you may find that your client may cling doggedly to wish to change the adversity at 'A'. If this happens, what can you do? I will focus here on the situation where your client wishes to change the behaviour of another person involved in the specific example.

Help your client to see the difference between changing another person and influencing that person

Help your client to see that there is a difference between changing another person and influencing that person. Help your client to understand that were you to accept the goal of changing the other person, you would be encouraging your client to change what is outside her direct control to change. Rather, help her to see that the other person's behaviour is under their direct control and not your client's.

If your client accepts this, show her that it does not mean there is nothing that she can do. Show her that she can influence that person to change and that as these attempts to influence the other person are under your client's direct control then they are acceptable as behavioural goals.

Help your client to understand that influencing another person is best done when she is not emotionally disturbed

Once your client has set 'attempts to influence the other person' as her behavioural goal, ask her whether her influence behaviours are more likely to be successful if she is in an emotionally disturbed frame of mind or if she is in an emotionally healthy frame of mind. Most clients can see that being in an emotionally healthy frame of mind will increase their chances of persuading the other person to change – without, of course, guaranteeing this outcome.

Case study: Linda

Here is how I responded to Linda in this goal-eliciting step when she continued to express a desire to get her boss to change his mind and promote her.

WINDY: So, instead of feeling unhealthily angry and feeling like shouting abuse at him and giving him a slap, what is your goal in this situation?

LINDA: To get him to change his mind.

[Windy's observation: Linda is focused on changing her boss rather than changing her responses, so let me address this issue.]

WINDY: Who is ultimately in charge of your boss's decision to promote you: him or you?

LINDA: Sadly, him.

WINDY: What are you in charge of with respect to, as you put it, 'getting him to change his mind'?

LINDA: I guess my own behaviour.

WINDY: You guessed right! ... (both laugh) ... So is feeling like shouting abuse at him and giving him a slap a good foundation for increasing the chances of influencing him to promote you?

LINDA (laughs): No.

WINDY: And what alternative behaviour would increase your chances?

LINDA: Being assertive with him and coming up with rational arguments as to why he should keep his promise to promote me.

WINDY: And will your feelings of unhealthy anger help you or hinder you in this respect?

LINDA: It will hinder me ... definitely.

WINDY: So you need a feeling that acknowledges the badness of your boss's broken promise to you and that helps you to assert yourself and give those rational arguments. Would you want to set that as your feeling goal?

LINDA: Sounds good.

WINDY: So what would you call that emotion? Remember it needs to be negative and acknowledges the badness of the broken promise, but it also needs to help you to be assertive and give rational arguments.

LINDA: I would like to call it being constructively annoyed.

WINDY: Rather than unhealthily angry?

LINDA: Yes.

[Windy's observation: It is important to use a client's language when referring to a HNE goal. Constructive annoyance is close enough to healthy anger to be acceptable, in my view.]

WINDY: So let me sum up. Rather than feel unhealthily angry with your boss for breaking his promise to you, you have set as your goal to feel constructively annoyed about the broken promise instead. While unhealthy anger leads you to want to shout abuse at your boss and slap him, an urge which fortunately you are able to suppress, constructive annoyance would help to actually assert yourself with him and allow you to provide rational arguments why he should change his mind back and keep his promise. However, you also recognize that all you can do is to control your own behaviour and you recognize that no matter how persuasive you may be, in the final analysis your boss is in charge of whether or not he chooses to promote you. Is that summary accurate?

LINDA: Very accurate.

Ways of eliciting an emotional goal

In therapy as in life, what you get is largely determined by how you go about trying to get it. This is especially true when it comes to eliciting your client's emotional goal. Let me review such strategies.

Ask for a goal in an open-ended way: using Linda as an example where appropriate

When you ask your client for an emotional goal, you simply refer to her goal without qualifying this in any way. Examples of such an approach are:

- what would like to achieve in discussing this example with me?
- what is your goal here?

These are open-ended questions and while they give your client freedom to express her goal in her own way, they are problematic in that such questions decrease the chances of you getting what you are looking for: an emotional response (to the adversity at 'A') that is negative and healthy and as such is a constructive alternative to your client's actual emotional response; which is both negative and unhealthy.

In outlining goal statements in response to the open-ended question, I will briefly comment on the problems with them and how to address them.

Thus, in response to such open-ended questions your client may say that she wants the following.

TO CHANGE THE OTHER PERSON

I have discussed the issues relevant to this on p. 91.

TO BE INDIFFERENT TO THE ADVERSITY (IN OTHER WORDS TO HAVE A NEUTRAL EMOTION)

Here Linda might say: 'My goal is not to care about not being promoted'.

This is only possible if Linda truly did not care about being promoted, but she does care and helping her to achieve the goal of indifference would encouraging her to lie to herself. Help your client to see this and that she needs to commit herself to feeling an emotion that reflects the fact that she does care about not getting want she wants, for example, but that does not reflect emotional disturbance.

TO CHANGE HER OWN BEHAVIOUR IN A CONSTRUCTIVE WAY WITHOUT MENTIONING A CHANGE IN EMOTION

Here, Linda might say: 'I want to assert myself with my boss'.

Help your client to see that her constructive behaviour is linked with a HNE. Help her to formulate this and give it a name that makes sense to her.

TO CHANGE THE SITUATION

Here Linda might say: 'I want to find another job'.

The trouble with this goal is that it is not focused on a healthy emotional response and thus is likely to be based on the same irrational belief that underpins her emotional problem in the first place. Help your client to see that such decisions are best taken when she is in a healthy frame of mind and for this to be achieved she needs to deal with her emotional problem, not bypass the problem or take a decision that is, in fact, based on the problem. As such, proceed to help her to set a healthy emotional goal in response to her adversity at 'A'.

TO CHANGE HER OWN BEHAVIOUR BUT IN AN UNCONSTRUCTIVE WAY

Here, Linda might say: 'I want to get back at my boss without him finding out about it'.

When your client comes up with a goal that is unconstructive, she may not initially realize that it is unconstructive. Thus, your first step is to help her to see that the goal is unconstructive. In Linda's case her behavioural goal (as stated above) is an expression of her unhealthy anger not a healthy alternative to it. After your client understands the dysfunctionality of her behavioural goal then you can begin to help her to construct a healthy one.

Ask for an emotional goal

When you ask your client for an emotional goal in the specific example, you are asking her to specify an emotion that she could have experienced that is different from the emotion that she did experience. Examples of such an approach are:

- how would you have liked to have felt in this situation?

- what would have been a more healthy emotion for you to have experienced in this situation?

DESIRED VERSUS HEALTHY EMOTIONAL GOALS

Note the differences between these two questions. The first asks the client to give her preference for an alternative emotion, while the second asks her to think about the healthiness of the alternative emotion. Both have their problems. In the first, the client may wish to experience an emotion that is not healthy, while in the second, the client may be able to specify a healthy emotional alternative, but not wish to experience it.

It follows, therefore, that if you ask for an emotional goal in response to the adversity at 'A', you need to ensure (1) that the client can specify a HNE that is a good alternative to the UNE she experienced in the specific example of her emotional problem, and (2) that she wants to experience this emotion.

SEEKING LESS OF A DISTURBED EMOTION

When you ask your client for her emotional goal in the selected specific example, in addition to her wanting to feel indifference or calm in the face of adversity (see above), she may opt to feel less of the disturbed emotion in question. On the face of it, this may seem quite reasonable. Thus, for example, if your client experiences strong anxiety in her selected specific example, what is wrong with her wanting to feel less of this painful emotion?

RECBT's position on the difference between UNEs and NHEs is that the former stem from irrational beliefs and the latter stem from rational beliefs (see Tables 1–8). As irrational beliefs are qualitatively rather than quantitatively different from rational beliefs (i.e. meaning they are on different continua not at the opposite ends of the same continuum), it follows that UNEs are qualitatively, not quantitatively different from HNEs. Thus, an HNE is on a different continuum from its UNE counterpart and not on opposite ends of the same continuum.

Since an HNE has its own continuum its health is not determined by its intensity but by the fact that it is underpinned by rational beliefs as I discussed earlier in the book (see p. 26). Thus, an HNE can be strong and healthy.

It follows from the above that if your client wants to feel less of a disturbed emotion, she will still be experiencing a disturbed emotion. If you accept this as a legitimate emotional goal, what you will, in effect, be doing is helping your client to strive to acquire a weaker version of the irrational belief that underpins her more intense UNE.

If your client does specify a less intense version of her UNE as her goal, you need to do the following.

1 Help her to see that a less intense disturbed emotion is still a disturbed emotion and is still linked to unconstructive overt behaviours and action tendencies.
2 Help her to set more constructive behavioural responses.
3 Help her to see that an HNE alternative to her UNE is associated with these constructive behavioural responses and that it can remain healthy even if it is a strong emotion.
4 Have her name the HNE and use this name subsequently in your work with her.

Eliciting an emotional goal based on an explanation of what you are looking for

So far I have discussed two strategies for eliciting your client's emotional goal in the selected specific example that were based on asking questions [(1) for a goal and (2) for an emotional goal]. In using both types of questions, you are not being clear about what you are looking for and thus, both are problematic and can lead you to deal with issues that you may not have had to deal with if you were clear about what you are looking for. Given this, I recommend that you use a strategy to elicit an emotional goal that is based more on explaining what you are looking for and why you are looking for it. As such, this strategy is more theory-driven than the two questioning strategies in that it is derived directly from the theory of RECBT concerning the difference between UNEs and HNEs.

Case study: Linda

Here is how I suggest using this explanation-based strategy. In doing so, I will show you how I would have used this strategy with Linda.

---

1 Review what you have already identified with respect to your client's specific example and write the resulting 'situational ABC' on a white board under the heading 'Problem' to remind your client that this 'situational ABC' relates to a specific example of her emotional problem. Thus, with Linda I would have written the following.

Problem

Situation
Going to see my boss in his office at lunchtime to talk about me not being promoted

'A'
My boss broke his promise to me

'B'
Not yet assessed

'C'
Emotional C: Unhealthy anger
Behavioural 'C': Feeling like shouting abuse at him and giving him a slap.

---

2 Explain that the situation is not going to change. In Linda's case, the reality is that she is going into the boss's office at lunchtime to discuss with him the fact that she was not promoted.

3 Encourage her to continue to assume temporarily that her 'A' was correct since she was reacting to it as though it were true in the specific example of her

emotional problem and thus, if she is to respond to it more constructively, she needs to continue to assume 'A' is true, albeit again temporarily. In Linda's case I would have encouraged her to continue to assume that her boss had broken his promise to her in order to help her to deal with this in a healthier way.

4 Help her to see the only things that she can change are her emotional and behavioural 'C's' and her thinking 'C' (if you have identified this 'C' as well). Summarize this in another goal-oriented 'situational ABC' – which I suggest that you put next to the problem-based 'situational ABC' – under the heading 'Goal'. Thus, with Linda, I would have written the following.

Problem	Goal
Situation	*Situation*
Going to see my boss in his office at lunchtime to talk about me not being promoted	Going to see my boss in his office at lunchtime to talk about me not being promoted
'*A*'	'*A*'
My boss broke his promise to me	My boss broke his promise to me
'*B*'	'*B*'
Not yet assessed	Not yet assessed
'*C*'	'*C*'
Emotional 'C': Unhealthy anger	Emotional 'C' goal: Alternative emotion – (healthy and negative)
Behavioural 'C': Feeling like shouting abuse at him and giving him a slap	Behavioural 'C' goal: Alternative overt behaviour or action tendency – (constructive)

At this point you can either focus on your client's behavioural response to 'A' or on her emotional response to 'A'. As I focused first on Linda's behavioural response, I will start with that.

5 Have your client focus on her problematic behavioural response to 'A' and ask her what the consequences of her overt behaviour were (or would be) or what the impact of suppressing her action tendencies was (or would be). Once your client recognizes the negative consequence of her overt behaviour and the negative impact of her suppressed action tendencies ask her what behavioural response would be (1) realistic, (2) healthy, and (3) acceptable to her. Stress that a realistic behavioural response is one that reflects the negativity of the 'A', a healthy response is one that is in the person's short- and long-term interests and an acceptable response is one to which the person can commit to implementing.

In Linda's case, I would have helped her to choose 'asserting myself with my boss and advancing rational arguments to encourage him to keep his promise to promote me' as her behavioural goal since she considered that it met the three criteria of realism, health and acceptability.

6 You are now in a position to help the client to construct an emotional goal. This emotion should also meet the criteria of realism, health and acceptability. Thus, the emotion should realistically be negative given that the 'A' to which it is a response is negative. As a rule of thumb the intensity of this emotion should reflect how negatively your client sees 'A'. The more negatively she views 'A' the stronger her HNE will be. The emotion should be healthy in that it should be in the person's healthy interests and accompany and facilitate her behavioural response discussed above. Finally, it should be one to which the client can commit to experiencing

and in this sense it should also have a name that is acceptable to the client.

Linda chose 'constructive annoyance' as her emotional goal in that it made sense to her, she could see it was healthy and would help her to assert herself and express rational reasons why her boss should ideally keep his promise to promote her. It was also a realistic response to her boss breaking his promise to her and the strength of the emotion matched negative evaluation of 'A'.

We are now in a position to present Linda's completed problem and goal 'situational ABC' below.

Problem	Goal
Situation	*Situation*
Going to see my boss in his office at lunchtime to talk about me not being promoted	Going to see my boss in his office at lunchtime to talk about me not being promoted
'*A*'	'*A*'
My boss broke his promise to me	My boss broke his promise to me
'*B*'	'*B*'
Not yet assessed	Not yet assessed
'*C*'	'*C*'
Emotional 'C': Unhealthy anger	Emotional 'C' goal: Constructive annoyance
Behavioural 'C': Feeling like shouting abuse at him and giving him a slap	Behavioural 'C' goal: Asserting myself with my boss and advancing rational reasons to encourage him to keep his promise to support me

Step 10: help your client to understand the 'B'–'C' connection

When working on the specific example of your client's emotional problem, you have identified the following:

- the situation in which it occurred
- her disturbed emotion and unconstructive behaviour (and perhaps even her highly distorted subsequent thinking), all of which occur at 'C'
- what she found most disturbing in the situation that is her adversity at 'A'
- her emotional and behavioural goals (and perhaps even her thinking goals) that represent realistic and healthy ways of responding to which she is willing to commit.

The next step is to help her to understand what we in RECBT call the 'B'–'C' connection; which is the heart of RECBT. By helping your client grasp this connection, you are helping her to understand that the adversity she was or will be facing at 'A' does not determine her responses at 'C', rather it is the beliefs that she holds about the adversity that largely underpin these responses.

Three ways of making the 'B'–'C' connection

There are a number of ways of doing this. Below are three options.

Ask your client whether 'C' is determined by 'A' or by 'B'

In the first, you merely ask your client whether she thinks her UNE at 'C' is determined by the adversity at 'A' or by her beliefs at 'B'. Here is how I would have used this method with Linda.

Case study: Linda

> WINDY: So, Linda, we now know that you feel unhealth-
> ily angry towards your boss for breaking his

> promise towards you by not promoting you. Right?
>
> LINDA: Right.
>
> WINDY: But what largely determines your unhealthy anger, his broken promise or your belief about his broken promise?
>
> LINDA: Well, I'm tempted to say his broken promise because then I can blame him, but if I am honest, I guess it's my belief about his broken promise.

If, in her answer, your client shows that she understands the 'B'–'C' connection (as Linda did) then you can proceed to the next step. If not, you can use the following method known as the 100-person technique.

The 100-person technique

When you use the 100-person technique, you ask your client would a hundred people of the client's age and gender all experience the same UNE towards the same adversity. Hopefully the client will say 'no' at which point you can ask what would determine their different feelings about the same adversity. Work with your client until you have helped her to understand the 'B'–'C' connection. Here is how I would have used this technique with Linda.

Case study: Linda

> WINDY: Let me put this another way, would a hundred people of your age and gender all feel unhealthily angry towards their boss for breaking his or her promise to them?
>
> LINDA: I guess not, no.
>
> WINDY: What would account for their different feelings about the same adversity?

LINDA: Well, I suppose the way they looked at it.
WINDY: That's right. We say in this approach to coaching that your emotions are largely determined
by your beliefs, so the next step is for us to figure out the beliefs that underpin your feelings
of unhealthy anger.

The theory-driven 'B'–'C' technique

The third technique that I will discuss to facilitate client understanding of the 'B'–'C' connection is a theory-driven one. In this method you are in fact trying to achieve two things. Primarily, you are to teach the RECBT view that your client's UNE is largely determined by an irrational belief and her HNE alternative is largely determined by a rational belief. If your client understands what may be called the 'iB'–UNE connection and the 'rB'–HNE connection, she is also by implication understanding the more general 'B'–'C' connection. I favour theory-derived interventions in RECBT because they are time-efficient. Clients seem to get the point more quickly with theory-derived interventions than with more open-ended interventions, although this is a matter for research to test.

Case study: Linda
Here is how I would have used this technique with Linda.

WINDY: Let me outline two beliefs and you can tell me
which of the two would lead to your feelings of
unhealthy anger:

1 my boss absolutely should not have broken
his promise to promote me. He is a bad person for doing so
2 I would much prefer it if my boss had not
broken his promise to me, but sadly and

> regretfully there is no reason to state that he absolutely should not have done so. He is not a bad person, but a fallible one who has done a very bad thing.
>
> *LINDA:* The first one.
> *WINDY:* And what emotion would the second belief lead to?
> *LINDA:* What I have been calling constructive annoyance.
> *WINDY:* So can you see that it's not your boss's broken promise on its own that leads to your feelings of unhealthy anger but your rigid and other-depreciating belief about his broken promise?
> *LINDA:* Yes, I can see that.
> *WINDY:* And also can you see that if you hold a flexible and other-accepting belief about him breaking his promise then you will feel constructive annoyance and not unhealthy anger.

The purpose of *this* step is to establish the 'B'–'C' connection. The purpose of the *next* step is to establish the 'iB'–unhealthy 'C' connection. And the 'rB'–healthy 'C' connection. Note that if you used the last, theory-driven method you will have already done this.

Step 11: identify 'iBs', teach 'rBs' and make the appropriate connections with 'C'

I will assume that in the previous step you helped your client to understand the general 'B'–'C' connection, namely that her beliefs about adversities underpin her feelings. You are now ready, if you have not already have done so, to help her to identify the irrational beliefs (at 'B') that underpinned her UNE at 'C' and to help her make the 'iB'–'C' connection. You also need to help your client to understand what her alternative rational beliefs are and that they underpin her emotional goals (what is called the 'rB'–emotional goal connection).

An important reminder

Before I consider how you can do this, let me remind you of two points.

Eight unhealthy emotions and their healthy alternatives

You need a working grasp of the eight UNEs that clients often get stuck with and their healthy alternatives, if you are to help your client develop a plausible alternative to her emotional problem.

Unhealthy negative emotion	Healthy negative emotion
Anxiety	Concern
Depression	Sadness
Guilt	Remorse
Shame	Disappointment
Hurt	Sorrow
Unhealthy anger	Healthy anger
Unhealthy jealousy	Healthy jealousy
Unhealthy envy	Healthy envy

Please note that this list reflects the terminology that I tend to use. It is more important that you develop a shared language with your client on this issue than to employ my language. The main point to bear in mind is that you need to engage your client in a brief discussion concerning what constitutes a healthy alternative to her UNE given that her 'A' is an adversity.

Four irrational beliefs and their rational belief alternatives

You need to have a good working knowledge of the four irrational beliefs that underpin the above emotional problems and the four rational belief alternatives that, in turn, underpin the solutions to these problems. This material is summarized below.

Irrational beliefs	Rational beliefs
Demand	*Non-dogmatic preference*
X must (or must not) happen	I would like X to happen (or not happen), but it does not have to be the way I want it to be
Awfulizing belief	*Non-awfulizing belief*
It would be terrible if X happens (or does not happen)	It would be bad, but not terrible if X happens (or does not happen)
Discomfort intolerance belief	*Discomfort tolerance belief*
I could not bear it if X happens (or does not happen)	It would be difficult to bear if X happens (or does not happen), but I could bear it and it would be worth it to me to do so
Depreciation beliefs	*Acceptance belief*
If X happens (or does not happen) I am no good, you are no good, life is no good	If X happens (or does not happen), it does not prove that I am no good, you are no good, life is no good. Rather, I am a fallible human being, you are a fallible human being, life is a complex mixture of good, bad and neutral

While, there are four irrational beliefs, my view is that you often do not have time to identify and deal with all of them. Thus, my suggestion is that when identifying the irrational beliefs that account for the specific example of your client's emotional problem help your client to identify her rigid demand and the one other secondary irrational belief that accounted for her UNE in the selected example. Then help her to identify the non-dogmatic preference and the one rational belief that is the alternative selected secondary irrational belief.

In what follows, I will focus on rigid demands and non-dogmatic preferences. Please note that when you come to assess the demands in particular and you want to use the word 'should' make sure that you qualify it with the term 'absolutely'. In REBT theory only absolute shoulds lead to emotional disturbance.

Identify the rigid demand, teach the non-dogmatic preference and make the appropriate connections with 'C' and the emotional goal

There are a number of strategies that you can use to assess your client's demand and non-dogmatic preference relevant to the specific example of her emotional problem and her stated emotional goal. I will cover three in this section.

Open-ended enquiry

When you employ the open-ended strategy, you ask a question such as: 'What were you telling yourself about your boss breaking his promise to you that led you to feel unhealthily angry?'.

The main disadvantage of this open-ended question is that the client will give you another inference rather than an irrational belief. If so, help her to understand this and explain about irrational beliefs.

Case study: Linda

WINDY: What do you think you will tell yourself about your boss breaking his promise to you that will lead you to feel unhealthily angry when you go to see him?

LINDA: That he acted unfairly.

[Windy's observation: Here Linda has provided me with another inference rather than the irrational belief I am looking for. I will tell her this and explain about irrational beliefs.]

WINDY: Your boss acting unfairly is another interpretation like him breaking his promise to you. In this approach, we argue that unhealthy anger stems from a demand that you are making about your boss's broken promise rather than from the interpretation of the broken promise itself. Now when you feel unhealthily angry about his broken promise what demand will you be making?

LINDA: That he should not have broken his promise to me.

WINDY: In an absolute sense?

LINDA: Yes.

As you see from the above exchange, what I asked used the open-ended strategy and asked Linda what she will tell herself at 'B' about her adversity at 'A' to produce 'C', and she gave me another inference at 'A'. This is the problem with this strategy. You will find that if you use it, then your client may well not give you the irrational belief that you are looking for. Eventually, you will have to, as I did in the example with Linda, explain what you are looking for. This is why I do not particularly recommend you using the open-ended strategy with your clients. It does not help your client to look for her irrational belief, but will give you other things that she was thinking at the time or synonyms for inference at 'A'.

Another problem with the open-ended enquiry is that on its own, it does not help you to teach your client what alternative rational belief she would have to hold in order to achieve her emotional goal. You will probably have to teach her this 'rB'–emotional goal connection as well (see below).

WINDY: Well, we know that your goal is to feel constructively annoyed rather than unhealthily angry about your boss breaking his promise to promote you. Is that correct?

LINDA: That's right.

WINDY: What do you think you will tell yourself about your boss breaking his promise to you that will lead you to feel constructively annoyed rather than unhealthily angry when you go to see him?

LINDA: That there is probably a good reason for him acting unfairly.

[Windy's observation: Because I am not focusing Linda's attention on her non-dogmatic preference, she gives me an inference that puts a positive slant on her boss's behaviour. In RECBT, we argue that this is changing the 'A' and in doing so, Linda is depriving herself of an opportunity of changing her demand to a non-dogmatic preference while focusing on the boss breaking his promise and not on the possible good reason for him doing so. My task here, therefore, is to redirect Linda's attention back to her boss breaking his promise.]

WINDY: Possibly, but let's keep your focus on your boss breaking his promise rather than on any possible good reason he had for doing so. How could you make yourself constructively annoyed rather than unhealthily angry about him breaking his promise?

LINDA: By telling myself that he was probably under pressure from his boss.

[Windy's observation: Again, Linda is attempting to change her feeling by changing the 'A' once more by excusing the boss. This is a more specific version of her last attempt to feel annoyed. As it does not seem that Linda is going to change her emotion by changing her belief, I am going to have to teach her how to do this.]

WINDY: OK you are trying to change your feeling by again coming up with a plausible reason for your boss's behaviour rather than changing your belief. Let me see if I can help you more here. In this approach, we argue that constructive annoyance stems from your desire for your boss not to break his promise to you, but also a recognition that he doesn't have to do what you want him to do. Now can you see that if you hold this non-dogmatic preference that you will feel constructively annoyed rather than unhealthily angry?

LINDA: Yes, I can see that.

WINDY: Excellent.

The theory-driven enquiry: using Linda as an example

When you implement the theory-driven enquiry to identify your client's irrational belief, you are using REBT theory to inform the questions that you ask your client. Using this strategy, I would ask Linda the following question: 'When you see your boss in his office, what demand will you be making about his broken promise to make yourself unhealthily angry?'

You will see that by asking for the client's demand you are using REBT theory to inform the question for this theory states that unhealthily anger is based on a rigid demand (as are other UNEs).

If you use this theory-derived question you need to ensure that you are not putting words into your client's mouth. To guard against this, ask her to restate the demand in her own words if you think that this may be the case.

When you use the theory-driven enquiry to teach your client what her alternative rational belief would be, you will have to ask her a question such as the one I would have asked Linda: 'When you see your boss in his office, what do you wish but not demand that he had done with respect to his broken promise to make yourself constructively annoyed, rather than unhealthily angry?'.

You will see once more that by asking for the client's non-dogmatic preference you are again using REBT theory to inform the question, for this theory states that constructive annoyance is based on a non-dogmatic preference (as are other HNEs).

As before, if you use this theory-derived question you need to ensure that you are not putting words into your client's mouth. To guard against this, ask her to restate the non-dogmatic preference in her own words if you think that this may be the case. When doing so, ensure that your client asserts her preference (e.g. 'I would prefer my boss not to have broken his promise to promote me . . .') and keeps the belief flexible by negating her demand (e.g. '. . . but he does not have to do what I want him to do').

The theory-driven choice enquiry: Windy's preferred strategy

When you use the theory-drive choice enquiry approach you do the following:

- stress (1) that it is important to her that the adversity at 'A' does not happen or (2) that something desirable that has occurred does happen
- show her that she is either holding an irrational belief about the adversity or a rational belief
- ask her when she feels her UNE at 'C', is she holding the irrational belief or the rational belief?
- work with her until she understands that her UNE is underpinned by the irrational belief
- ask her to imagine that she is holding the rational belief instead and enquire how this would change her emotion
- work with her until she understands the link between her alternative rational belief and her emotional goal.

This approach is different from the theory-driven enquiry approach described above in that it keeps the rational and irrational beliefs together and the client is asked to choose which one underpins her emotional problem and which underpins her emotional goal. In the theory-driven enquiry approach, the irrational belief is introduced first before the rational belief

Case study: Linda
Let me show you how I used the theory-driven choice enquiry approach with Linda.

WINDY: Ok, Linda, I want to see if I can understand and help you to understand the belief that accounts for your unhealthy anger about your boss's broken promise to you. Now we know it was important to you that he did not break his promise. Correct?

LINDA: Correct.

WINDY: Now, given that, your belief could go one of two ways. I want to put these two beliefs to you so that you can identify which belief would underpin your unhealthy anger when you see your boss. OK?

LINDA: OK.

WINDY: Good, Here's belief Number 1: 'It's important to me that my boss not break his promise to promote me and therefore he absolutely should not have done so'. Now here is belief Number 2: 'It's important to me that my boss not break his promise to promote me, but sadly and regretfully he does not have to do what I want him to do'.

　　　　　Which belief would underpin your unhealthy anger at the time when you experience it?

LINDA: Belief Number 1.

> *WINDY:*   And which belief would lead you to feel con-
> structively annoyed about the broken promise
> rather than unhealthy anger?
> *LINDA:*   Belief Number 2.

I particularly recommend this strategy because it simultaneously helps your client to see that a rigid, irrational
belief underpins her emotional problem and that a flexible
rational belief underpins her emotional solution.

Identify extreme beliefs and teach non-extreme beliefs

Once you have identified your client's demand and related
non-dogmatic preference, you can teach her the other three
irrational beliefs and the alternative rational beliefs and
ask her to choose the one other irrational belief that best
accounted for her UNE at 'C' (and by implication the
alternative rational belief that will help her to achieve her
goals).

Case study: Linda

Let me end this step, by showing how I used the theory-
driven choice enquiry approach to identify Linda's depreciation belief and alternative acceptance belief.

> *WINDY:*   OK, Linda, now as you anticipate feeling un-
> healthy anger towards your boss for break-
> ing his promise to support you, I want to see if I
> can understand and help you to understand the
> belief towards your boss that stems from your
> demand and accounts for your unhealthy anger
> towards him. Now we know that you think that
> it is bad that your boss broke his promise to
> promote you, but when you are unhealthily

> angry, do you believe that he is bad for acting
> badly or do you believe that he is not bad, but a
> fallible human being for acting badly?
> *LINDA:* I believe he is bad.
> *WINDY:* And how would you feel if you believe that he
> is not bad, but a fallible human being for acting
> badly?
> *LINDA:* Constructively annoyed.

Now that I have helped Linda to see the link between her irrational beliefs (demand and other-depreciation belief) and her unhealthy anger, on the one hand and the link between her rational belief (non-dogmatic preference and other-acceptance belief) and her constructive annoyance, on the other, she is ready to make a commitment to pursue her emotional and/or behavioural goals and to see that changing her irrational beliefs is the best way of doing this. In the next step, I will show how you can elicit this commitment.

Step 12: elicit commitment from the client to pursue her emotional and/or behavioural goals and help her to see that changing her irrational beliefs is the best way of doing this

I have stressed in this practical sequence that it is very important for you to engage your client in a discussion concerning what constitutes a healthy alternative to her emotional problem (UNE and/or dysfunctional behaviour) at 'C'. However, such an appreciation has to be backed up by your client making a commitment to work towards this healthy emotion/functional behaviour. In this step, I will discuss how you can elicit such a commitment together with an understanding that the best way your client can achieve her goals is to change her irrational beliefs.

Dealing with your client's doubts, reservations and objections to committing herself to her emotional goals

As you do this you may need to identify and respond to your client's doubts, reservations and objections to this new 'C'. Let me illustrate what I mean.

Case study: Linda

> *WINDY:* OK, Linda, so you can see that your demand and other-depreciation belief underpin your unhealthy anger towards your boss and that your non-dogmatic preference and your other-acceptance belief underpin your feelings of constructive annoyance. So if you want to feel constructively annoyed instead of unhealthily angry towards your boss what do you need to change?
> *LINDA:* My irrational beliefs.
> *WINDY:* Would you like to make a commitment to doing

> this or do you have some doubts or reservations about doing so?
>
> *LINDA:* Well, I have one reservation.
>
> *WINDY:* What's that?
>
> *LINDA:* If I am constructively annoyed then my feelings will be light and won't reflect the badness of what my boss did to me.
>
> *[Windy's observation: This is a common misconception about healthy negative feelings that clients have. In reality, because rational beliefs can be strongly held and reflect the importance of what your client wants, but does not demand, an HNE can vary in intensity according to this level of importance. Thus, constructive annoyance can be mild, moderate or strong depending upon how important your client's non-dogmatic preference is.]*
>
> *WINDY:* Not necessarily. For example, if your rational belief is as follows: 'I mildly want my boss to keep his promise, but he does not have to do so', then the intensity of your constructive annoyance will be mild or light if he breaks his promise. If your belief is: 'I moderately want my boss to keep his promise, but he does not have to do so', then your constructive annoyance will be moderate if he breaks his promise. And finally, if your belief is: 'I very strongly want my boss to keep his promise, but he still does not have to do so', then your constructive annoyance is very strong when your boss breaks his promise. So, you see, your constructive annoyance can reflect the badness of what your boss did as long as your non-dogmatic preference is strong. Does that answer your reservation?
>
> *LINDA:* Very much so.

Dealing with your client's wish to change 'A'

When you ask your client to commit herself to pursuing her emotional goals about 'A', she may still say that she wants to change 'A' first. If so, you need to explain to your client that the best time to change 'A' is when she is not disturbed about 'A' and that her disturbance about 'A' will interfere with her change attempts. Once she understands this and that the best way to be undisturbed about 'A' is by thinking rationally about it, she is ready to question her irrational beliefs about 'A'. Here is how to intervene when your client's disturbance is largely emotional in nature.

Case study: Linda

WINDY: Is it best to change your boss's mind about not giving you the promised promotion when you are feeling unhealthily angry (UNE) or when you are feeling constructively annoyed (HNE)?

LINDA: When I feel constructively annoyed.

[Windy's observation: If Linda had said her unhealthy anger (i.e. her UNE), I would have endeavoured to discover the reasons for her response and then correct any misconceptions that I found.]

WINDY: And based on what we have discussed what do you need to change in order to feel constructively annoyed (HNE), but not unhealthy anger (UNE) about your boss breaking his promise to you?

LINDA: My irrational belief.

[Windy's observation: I would have intervened if she gave any other answer, one again eliciting her reasons and then correcting any misconceptions she expressed.]

WINDY: And are you committed to do this before trying to get him to change his mind?

LINDA: Yes.

Your client is now ready to question her irrational and rational beliefs.

Step 13: question both irrational and rational beliefs: choosing a strategy

When you question your client's beliefs (both irrational and rational) your goal is to help her see that her irrational beliefs are irrational and her rational beliefs are rational. This is known as intellectual insight because while the client understands this point, she does not yet have deep conviction in it to the extent that it influences, for the better, her feelings and behaviour. This 'emotional insight' will come about later in the process, when you help her to strengthen her conviction in her rational belief and weaken her conviction in her rational belief.

The following list shows the characteristics of both irrational and rational beliefs and you should employ these characteristics in your questioning.

Irrational beliefs	Rational beliefs
Rigid or extreme	Flexible or non-extreme
False	True
Illogical	Logical
Leads to unconstructive results	Leads to constructive results

For your client to achieve such intellectual insight, she has to question both her irrational beliefs and her rational beliefs.

Please note that I suggest that you question your client's demand and non-dogmatic preference (unless there is a good reason not to) and the one other irrational belief and rational belief that your client can see is the most appropriate derivative from the demand and non-dogmatic preference respectively.

Strategies in questioning the client's irrational and rational belief

Given that time is often at a premium in life coaching, I recommend that you help your client question one irrational belief and one rational belief at a time, but to do so together. Compare this to two other strategies:

Strategy 1: Question the relevant irrational and rational belief together (Windy's preferred approach):

Question the demand and the alternative non-dogmatic preference
then
Question the awfulizing belief and the alternative non-awfulizing belief
or
Question the discomfort intolerance belief and the alternative discomfort tolerance belief
or
Question the depreciation belief and the alternative acceptance belief.

Strategy 2: Question the irrational belief and then the alternative rational belief separately:

Question the demand
then
Question the alternative full preference
and
Question the awfulizing belief
then
Question the alternative non-awfulizing belief
or
Question the discomfort intolerance belief
then
Question the alternative discomfort tolerance belief
or
Question the depreciation belief
then
Question the alternative acceptance belief.

Strategy 3: Question all relevant irrational beliefs first and then their rational belief alternatives:

Question the demand
and
Question the awfulizing belief
or
Question the discomfort intolerance belief
or
Question the depreciation belief
then
Question the alternative non-dogmatic preference
or
Question the alternative non-awfulizing belief
and
Question the alternative discomfort tolerance belief
or
Question the alternative acceptance belief.

In this book, I will present material based on my preferred strategy that involves questioning the relevant irrational and rational belief together (Steps 14–17). If you favour one of the other two strategies proceed accordingly. You can still benefit from using this guide, but may have to make an additional effort to find the appropriate material.

Before I proceed, I wish to make the point again that you often do not have the time to question all four irrational and rational beliefs (if indeed your client holds all four). I suggest that you help your client question *separately* her demand/non-dogmatic preference and the one other irrational/rational belief that she resonates with. This is very important so I will repeat it.

> Help your client question *separately* her demand/non-dogmatic preference and the one other irrational/rational belief that she resonates with.

One final point, before I consider how to question your client's beliefs (both irrational and rational). As you proceed with questioning her beliefs, you should note which points she finds particularly persuasive concerning seeing that her irrational beliefs are irrational and her rational beliefs are rational. Note these arguments and capitalize on them as you proceed.

Step 14: question a demand and a non-dogmatic preference

Demand	Non-dogmatic preference
X must (or must not) happen	I would like X to happen (or not happen), but it does not have to be the way I want it to be

I recommend that you use three main questions when questioning your client's demand and non-dogmatic preference: the empirical question, the logical question and the pragmatic question. Then, you can ask which belief the client wants to strengthen and which she wants to weaken and why.

First, help your client to focus on her demand and her non-dogmatic preference alternative. Have her write it down side by side (as above) or write it down yourself on a white board (again as above). Then move on to the three questions, I will present them in a certain sequence. This sequence is only a guide and other sequences are fine.

The empirical question

> WINDY: Which of the following beliefs is true and which is false and why?
>
> Demand ('iB'): My boss absolutely should not have broken his promise to promote me.
>
> Non-dogmatic preference ('rB'): It's important to me that my boss not break his promise to promote me, but sadly and regretfully he does not have to do what I want him to do.

According to REBT theory, the only correct answer to this question is that the non-dogmatic preference is true and the demand is false. Help your client understand the following.

- A rigid demand is inconsistent with reality. For such a demand to be true the demanded conditions would already have to exist when they do not. Or as soon as the client makes her demand then these demanded conditions would have to come into existence. Both positions are patently inconsistent with reality.
- On the other hand, a non-dogmatic preference is true since its two component parts are true. Your client can prove that she has a particular desire and can provide reasons why she wants what she wants. She can also prove that she does not have to get what she desires.

If your client gives you any other answer then help her through discussion to see why her answer is incorrect and help her to accept the correct answer.

The logical question

> *WINDY:* Which of the following beliefs is logical and which is illogical and why?
>
> Demand ('iB'): My boss absolutely should not have broken his promise to promote me.
>
> Non-dogmatic preference ('rB'): It's important to me that my boss not break his promise to promote me, but sadly and regretfully he does not have to do what I want him to do.

Your client needs to acknowledge that her demand is illogical while her non-dogmatic preference is logical. Help her to see that her demand is based on the same desire as her non-dogmatic preference, but that she transforms it as follows. Here is Linda's transformation:

> It's important to me that my boss not break his promise to promote me . . . and therefore he absolutely should not have done so.

Show her that this belief has two components. The first ['It's important to me that my boss not break his promise to promote me . . .] is not rigid, but the second [. . . and therefore he absolutely should not have done so] is rigid. As such her rigid demand isn't logical since one cannot logically derive something rigid from something that is not rigid. Use the template in Figure 1 with your client to illustrate this visually, if necessary.

Linda's non-dogmatic preference is as follows:

> It's important to me that my boss not break his promise to promote me . . . but sadly and regretfully he does not have to do what I want him to do.

Her non-dogmatic preference is logical since both parts are not rigid and thus the second component logically follows

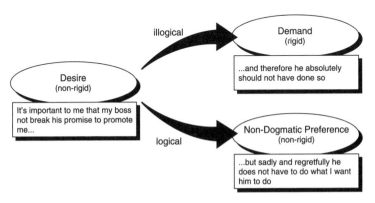

Figure 1 **A demand is illogical and a non-dogmatic preference is logical.**

from the first. Again, use the template in Figure 1 with your client to illustrate this visually, if necessary.

If your client gives you any other answer then help her through discussion to see why her answer is incorrect and help her to accept the correct answer.

The pragmatic question

> WINDY: Which of the following beliefs leads to largely good results and which leads to largely poor results and why?
>
> Demand ('iB'): My boss absolutely should not have broken his promise to promote me.
>
> Non-dogmatic preference ('rB'): It's important to me that my boss not break his promise to promote me, but sadly and regretfully he does not have to do what I want him to do.

You need to help your client acknowledge that her demand leads to unhealthy results for her, while her non-dogmatic preference leads to healthier results. As you do this, use the information provided by your client when you discussed the 'iB'–'C', 'rB'–emotional goal connections (see Step 11, pp. 106–115).

If your client thinks that her demand leads to healthier consequences than her non-dogmatic preference, help her through discussion to see why she is likely to be wrong.

Assess the client's commitment to belief change

You can then assess your client's commitment to changing her belief by asking a question such as:

> Which belief do you want to strengthen and which do you want to weaken and why?

After the questioning you have undertaken, your client 'should' indicate that she wishes to work to strengthen her conviction in her non-dogmatic preference and to weaken her conviction in her demand and be able to give coherent reasons why based on her problematic feelings and behaviour and her goals for change. If your client gives you any other answer then discover the reasons for this answer and work with her until she states a genuine commitment to the non-dogmatic preference.

As part of assessing such commitment, it is worth asking your client whether she has any doubts, reservations and objections to strengthening her non-dogmatic preference and weakening her demand. If she has any such doubts, respond to them with tact, and until your client has relinquished her reservations. See Dryden (2001) for a fuller discussion of this issue.

Case study: Linda

I will discuss my questioning of Linda's demand and non-dogmatic preference in Part 4.

Step 15: question an awfulizing and a non-awfulizing belief

Awfulizing belief	Non-awfulizing belief
It would be terrible if X happens (or does not happen)	It would be bad, but not terrible if X happens (or does not happen)

When questioning your client's awfulizing and non-awfulizing beliefs use the same three questions that you used to question her demands and non-dogmatic preferences: i.e. the empirical question, the logical question and the pragmatic question. Once you have done this you can then ask which belief the client wants to strengthen and which she wants to weaken and why.

First, help your client to focus on her awfulizing belief and her non-awfulizing belief alternative. Again ask her to write it down side by side (as above) or write it down yourself on a white board (again as above). Then move on to the three questions.

The empirical question

> *WINDY:* Which of the following beliefs is true and which is false and why?
>
> Awfulizing belief (iB): It is terrible that my boss broke his promise to promote me.
>
> Non-awfulizing belief (rB): It is bad that my boss broke his promise to promote me, but not terrible.

According to REBT theory, an awfulizing belief is false and a non-awfulizing belief is true.

When questioning your client's awfulizing belief help

your client to see that when she is holding this attitude, she believes the following:

• nothing could be worse
• the event in question is worse than 100% bad, and
• no good could possibly come from this bad event.

Help her to see that all three convictions are inconsistent with reality and that her non-awfulizing belief is true since this is made up of the following ideas:

• things could always be worse
• the event in question is less than 100% bad, and
• good could come from this bad event

If your client gives you answers that are at variance with the above then help her through discussion to see why her answers are incorrect and help her to accept the correct answer.

The logical question

> *WINDY:* Which of the following beliefs is logical and which is illogical and why?
>
> Awfulizing belief (iB): It is terrible that my boss broke his promise to promote me.
>
> Non-awfulizing belief (rB): It is bad that my boss broke his promise to promote me, but not terrible.

Help your client see that her awfulizing belief is illogical, while her non-awfulizing belief is logical. Show her that her awfulizing belief is based on the same evaluation of badness as her non-awfulizing belief, but she transforms this as follows:

> It is bad that my boss broke his promise to promote me
> ... and therefore it is terrible.

Show her that her awfulizing belief has two components. The first ('It is very bad that my boss broke his promise to promote me') is non-extreme, while the second (... and therefore it is terrible) is extreme. As such, help her to see that her awfulizing belief is illogical since one cannot logically derive something extreme from something that is not extreme. Use the template in Figure 2 with your client to illustrate this visually, if necessary.

Your client's non-awfulizing belief is as follows:

> It is bad that my boss broke his promise to promote
> me ... but it is not terrible.

Encourage your client to see that her non-awfulizing belief is logical since both parts are non-extreme and thus the second component logically follows from the first. Again, use the

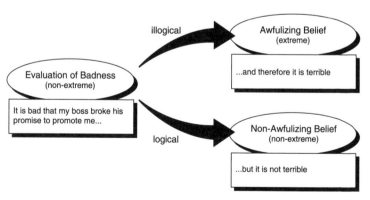

Figure 2 An awfulizing belief is illogical and a non-awfulizing belief is logical.

template in Figure 2 with your client to illustrate this visually, if necessary.

The pragmatic question

> *WINDY:*   Which of the following beliefs leads to largely good results and which leads to largely poor results and why?
>
> Awfulizing belief (iB): It is terrible that my boss broke his promise to promote me.
>
> Non-awfulizing belief (rB): It is bad that my boss broke his promise to promote me, but it is not terrible.

You need to help your client acknowledge that her awfulizing belief leads to unhealthy results for her, while her non-awfulizing belief leads to healthier results. As you do this, again use the information provided by your client when you discussed the 'iB'–'C', 'rB'–emotional goal connections (see Step 11, pp. 106–115).

If your client thinks that her awfulizing belief leads to healthier consequences than her non-awfulizing belief, help her through discussion to see why she is likely to be wrong.

Assess the client's commitment to belief change

You can then assess your client's commitment to changing her belief by asking a question such as:

> Which belief do you want to strengthen and which do you want to weaken and why?

After the questioning you have undertaken, your client

'should' indicate that she wishes to work to strengthen her conviction in her non-awfulizing belief and to weaken her conviction in her awfulizing belief and be able to give coherent reasons for her answer. If your client gives you any other answer then discover the reasons for this answer and work with her until she states a genuine commitment to her non-awfulizing belief.

Again as part of assessing such commitment, it is worth asking your client whether she has any doubts, reservations and objections to strengthening her non-awfulizing belief and weakening her awfulizing belief demand. If she has any such doubts, respond to them with tact, and until your client has relinquished her reservations (see Dryden, 2001).

Step 16: question a discomfort intolerance belief and a discomfort tolerance belief

Discomfort intolerance belief	Discomfort tolerance belief
I could not bear it if X happens (or does not happen)	It would be difficult to bear if X happens (or does not happen), but I could bear it and it would be worth it to me to do so

When questioning your client's discomfort intolerance belief and discomfort tolerance belief again use the tripartite questioning approach: the empirical question, the logical question and the pragmatic question. Once you have done this again ask which belief the client wants to strengthen and which she wants to weaken and why.

Once again begin by suggesting that your client focus on her discomfort intolerance belief and her discomfort tolerance alternative. Again, ask her to write it down side by side (as above) or write it down yourself on a white board (again as above). Then move on to the three questions.

The empirical question

> *WINDY:* Which of the following beliefs is true and which is false and why?
>
> Discomfort tolerance belief (iB): I can't bear it that my boss broke his promise to promote me.
>
> Discomfort tolerance belief (rB): It is hard for me to bear it that my boss broke his promise to promote me, but I can bear it and it is worth it to me to do so.

According to REBT theory, a discomfort tolerance belief is true and a discomfort intolerance belief is false.

When questioning your client's discomfort intolerance belief, help your client to see that when she is holding this attitude, she believes *at the time* the following:

- I will die or disintegrate if the frustration or discomfort continues to exist
- I will lose the capacity to experience happiness if the frustration or discomfort continues to exist.

Help her to see that both these convictions are inconsistent with reality and that her discomfort tolerance belief is true since this is made up of the following ideas:

- I will struggle if the frustration or discomfort continues to exist, but I will neither die nor disintegrate
- I will not lose the capacity to experience happiness if the frustration or discomfort continues to exist, although this capacity will be temporarily diminished, and
- the frustration or discomfort is worth tolerating.

If your client gives you answers that are at variance with the above then help her through discussion to see why her answers are incorrect and help her to accept the correct answer.

The logical question

> *WINDY:*   Which of the following beliefs is logical and which is illogical and why?
>
> Discomfort tolerance belief (iB): I can't bear it that my boss broke his promise to promote me.
>
> Discomfort tolerance belief (rB): It is hard for me to bear it that my boss broke his promise to promote me, but I can bear it and it is worth it to me to do so.

Help your client to see that her discomfort intolerance belief is illogical, while her discomfort tolerance belief is logical.

Show her that her discomfort intolerance belief is based on the same idea of struggle as her discomfort tolerance belief, but she transforms this as follows:

It is hard for me to bear it that my boss broke his promise to promote me . . . and therefore I can't bear it.

Show your client that her discomfort intolerance belief has two components. The first ('It is hard for me to bear it that my boss broke his promise to promote me ...') is non-extreme, while the second ('... and therefore I can't bear it') is extreme. As such help her to see that her discomfort intolerance belief is illogical since one cannot logically derive something extreme from something that is not extreme. Use the template in Figure 3 with your client to illustrate this visually, if necessary.

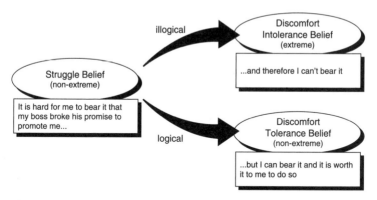

Figure 3 **A discomfort intolerance belief is illogical and a discomfort tolerance belief is logical.**

Your client's discomfort intolerance belief is as follows:

> It is hard for me to bear it that my boss broke his promise to promote me . . . but I can bear it and it is worth it to me to do so.

Encourage her to see that her discomfort tolerance belief is logical since both parts are non-extreme and thus the second component logically follows from the first. Again, use the template in Figure 3 with your client to illustrate this visually, if necessary.

The pragmatic question

> *WINDY:* Which of the following beliefs leads to largely good results and which leads to largely poor results and why?
>
> Discomfort tolerance belief (iB): I can't bear it that my boss broke his promise to promote me.
>
> Discomfort tolerance belief (rB): It is hard for me to bear it that my boss broke his promise to promote me, but I can bear it and it is worth it to me to do so.

You need to help your client acknowledge that her discomfort intolerance belief leads to unhealthy results for her, while her discomfort tolerance belief leads to healthier results. As you do this, once again use the information provided by your client when you discussed the 'iB'–'C', 'rB'–emotional goal connections if you need to (see Step 11, pp. 106–115).

Assess the client's commitment to belief change

You can then assess your client's commitment to changing her belief by asking a question such as:

> Which belief do you want to strengthen and which do you want to weaken and why?

After the questioning you have undertaken, your client 'should' indicate that she wishes to work to strengthen her conviction in her discomfort tolerance belief and to weaken her conviction in her discomfort intolerance belief and be able to give coherent reasons for her answer. If your client gives you any other answer then discover the reasons for this answer and work with her until she states a genuine commitment to her discomfort tolerance belief.

As part of assessing such commitment, it is worth asking your client once again whether she has any doubts, reservations and objections to strengthening her discomfort tolerance belief and weakening her discomfort intolerance belief. If she has any such doubts, respond to them with tact, and until your client has relinquished her reservations (see Dryden, 2001, for a fuller discussion of this issue).

Step 17: question a depreciation belief and an acceptance belief

Depreciation belief	Acceptance belief
If X happens (or does not happen) I am no good, you are no good, life is no good	If X happens (or does not happen), it does not prove that I am no good, you are no good, life is no good. Rather, I am a fallible human being, you are a fallible human being, life is a complex mixture of good, bad and neutral

When questioning your client's depreciation and acceptance beliefs once again use the following three questions: the empirical question, the logical question and the pragmatic question. As before, once you have done this again ask which belief the client wants to strengthen and which she wants to weaken and why.

Again suggest that your client focus on her depreciation belief and her acceptance belief alternative. Ask her to write it down side by side (as above) or write it down yourself on a white board (again as above). Then move on to the three questions.

The empirical question

> WINDY: Which of the following beliefs is true and which is false and why?
>
> Other-depreciation belief ('iB): It is bad that my boss broke his promise to promote me and therefore he is bad for doing so.
>
> Other-acceptance belief ('rB'): It is bad that my boss broke his promise to promote me, but he is not bad for doing so. He is a fallible human being who acted badly.

According to REBT theory, an acceptance belief is true and a depreciation belief is false.

Questioning your client's person-depreciation (self- or other-) belief

Help your client to see that when she is holding a person-depreciation belief (self- or other-), she believes *at the time* the following:

- a person (self or other) can legitimately be given a single global rating that defines their essence and the worth of a person is dependent upon conditions that change (e.g. my worth goes up when I do well and goes down when I don't do well)
- a person can be rated on the basis of one of his or her aspects.

Help her to see that these convictions are inconsistent with reality and that her person-acceptance (self- or other-) belief is true since this is made up of the following ideas:

- a person cannot legitimately be given a single global rating that defines their essence and their worth, as far as they have it, is not dependent upon conditions that change (e.g. my worth stays the same whether or not I do well)
- it makes sense to rate discrete aspects of a person, but it does not make sense to rate a person on the basis of these discrete aspects.

Questioning your client's life-depreciation belief

Help her to see that when she is holding a life-depreciation belief, she believes *at the time* the following:

- the world can legitimately be given a single rating that defines its essential nature and that the value of the world varies according to what happens within it (e.g. the value of the world goes up when something fair occurs and goes down when something unfair happens)
- the world can be rated on the basis of one of its aspects.

Help her to see that these convictions are inconsistent with reality and that her life-acceptance belief is true since this is made up of the following ideas:

- the world cannot legitimately be given a single rating that defines its essential nature and that the value of the world does not vary according to what happens within it (e.g. the value of the world stays the same whether fairness exists at any given time or not)
- it makes sense to rate discrete aspects of the world, but it does not make sense to rate the world on the basis of these discrete aspects.

If your client gives you answers that are at variance with the above then help her through discussion to see why her answers are incorrect and help her to accept the correct answer.

The logical question

> *WINDY:*   Which of the following beliefs is logical and which is illogical and why?
>
> Other-depreciation belief ('iB'): It is bad that my boss broke his promise to promote me and therefore he is bad for doing so.
>
> Other-acceptance belief ('rB'): It is bad that my boss broke his promise to promote me, but he is not bad for doing so. He is a fallible human being who acted badly.

Help your client see that her depreciation belief is illogical, while her acceptance belief is logical.

For example, you will see that Linda held an other-depreciation belief. So, I showed her that this belief was based on the same idea as her other-acceptance belief in that in both she acknowledged that it was bad that her boss broke his promise to promote her, but that in her other-depreciation belief she transformed it as follows:

> It is bad that my boss broke his promise to promote me
> . . . and therefore he is bad for doing so.

Thus, her other-depreciation belief has two components. The first (It is bad that my boss broke his promise to promote me . . .) is an evaluation of a part of her experience, while the second (. . . and therefore he is bad for doing so) is an evaluation of the whole of her boss's 'self'. As such, she is making the illogical part–whole error where the part is deemed illogically to define the whole.

Her other-acceptance belief is as follows:

> It is bad that my boss broke his promise to promote me . . . but he is not bad for doing so. He is a fallible human being who acted badly.

I encouraged Linda to see that her other-acceptance belief is logical because it shows that the 'self' of the other is complex and incorporates a bad event. Thus, in holding her other-acceptance belief she avoids making the part–whole error.

In helping your clients to question the logic of her depreciation and acceptance, remember the part–whole error and what constitutes its avoidance.

The pragmatic question

> *WINDY:* Which of the following beliefs leads to largely good results and which leads to largely poor results and why?
>
> Other-depreciation belief ('iB'): It is bad that my boss broke his promise to promote me and therefore he is bad for doing so.

Other-acceptance belief ('rB'): It is bad that my boss broke his promise to promote me, but he is not bad for doing so. He is a fallible human being who acted badly.

You need to help your client acknowledge that her depreciation belief leads to unhealthy results for her, while her acceptance belief leads to healthier results. As before, as you do this, use the information provided by your client when you discussed the 'iB'–'C', 'rB'–emotional goal connections if you need to (see Step 11, pp. 106–115).

Assess the client's commitment to belief change

You can then assess your client's commitment to changing her belief by asking a question such as:

Which belief do you want to strengthen and which do you want to weaken and why?

After the questioning you have undertaken, your client 'should' indicate that she wishes to work to strengthen her conviction in her acceptance belief and to weaken her conviction in her depreciation belief and be able to give coherent reasons for her answer. If your client gives you any other answer then discover the reasons for this answer and work with her until she states a genuine commitment to her acceptance belief.

As part of assessing such commitment, it is worth asking your client once again whether she has any doubts, reservations and objections to strengthening her acceptance belief and weakening her depreciation belief. If she has any such doubts, respond to them with tact, and until your client has relinquished her reservations (see Dryden, 2001, for a fuller discussion of this issue).

Case study: Linda

I will discuss my questioning of Linda's other-deprecation and other-acceptance beliefs in Part 4.

Step 18: help the client to strengthen her conviction in her rational beliefs and weaken her conviction in her irrational beliefs

I mentioned earlier in the book (see p. 119) that there are two types of insight in RECBT: intellectual insight and emotional insight.

When your client has intellectual insight, she understands why her irrational beliefs are irrational and why her rational beliefs are rational, but this insight has little impact on her feelings and behaviour. However, when your client has emotional insight, this understanding has great impact on her feelings and behaviour. In common parlance, when your client has intellectual insight into her irrational and rational beliefs, she can 'talk the talk', but when she has emotional insight into these beliefs, she can 'walk the talk'.

It is useful to explain to your client about these different forms of insight and what she needs to do to move from intellectual insight to emotional insight.

Explain the process of change

Here is an example of how to explain the process of change.

Case study: Linda

> *WINDY:* So now you can see that while you would have preferred your boss not to have broken his promise to promote you, sadly he does not have to do so and that he is not bad for doing so, but a fallible human being who did the wrong thing. But how much do you believe that right now?
>
> *LINDA:* Well, I can understand it, but I don't believe it.
>
> *WINDY:* What do you need to do to believe it?
>
> *LINDA:* I guess I need to practise the new belief and to act on it.

[Windy's observation: Linda has articulated the two main ingredients for change: practice and action.]

WINDY: Exactly, but bearing in mind that you have stronger conviction in your irrational beliefs than your rational beliefs even though you can see that they are irrational, how comfortable will you be when you do practise and act on your rational beliefs?

LINDA: I guess not that comfortable.

WINDY: That's right. And what would you need to do to be more comfortable with your rational beliefs?

LINDA: Keep practising them?

WINDY: That's right. Keep practising them and acting on them while tolerating the discomfort and as you do so your conviction in them will grow.

A selection of techniques to help your client gain conviction in her rational beliefs

There are a number of techniques that you can use to help your client to practise and act on her rational beliefs. I will review a few here and suggest that you consult Dryden (2001) if you are interested in learning more about such techniques.

Use the attack-response technique

This technique, which is sometimes called the zig-zag technique, is based on the idea that your client can strengthen her conviction in a rational belief by responding persuasively to attacks on this belief. I will outline the main (written) version of the attack-response technique, but there are also several variations on the same theme described more fully in Dryden (2001).

INSTRUCTIONS ON HOW TO TEACH YOUR CLIENT TO COMPLETE A
WRITTEN ATTACK-RESPONSE FORM

1 Ask your client to write down her specific rational belief on a piece of paper.

2 Ask her to rate her present level of conviction in this belief on a 100% point scale with 0% = no conviction and 100% = total conviction (i.e. your client really believes this in her gut and it markedly influences her feelings and behaviour). Ask her to write down this rating under her belief.

3 Ask your client to write down an attack on this rational belief. Her attack may take the form of a doubt, reservation or objection to this rational belief. It should also contain an explicit irrational belief (e.g. demand, awfulizing belief, discomfort tolerance belief or depreciation belief). Suggest that she make this attack as genuinely as she can. The more it reflects what she believes, the better.

4 Then tell your client to respond to this attack as fully as she can. It is really important that she responds to each element of the attack. In particular, make sure that she responds to irrational belief statements and also to distorted or unrealistic inferences framed in the form of a doubt, reservation or objection to the rational belief. Encourage her to do so as persuasively as possible and to write down her response.

5 Tell your client to continue in this vein until she has answered all of her attacks and cannot think of any more. Make sure throughout this process that she keeps the focus on the rational belief that she is trying to strengthen.

If your client finds this exercise difficult, suggest that she makes it easier by making her attacks gently at first. Then, when she finds that she can respond to these attacks quite easily, suggest that she begins to make the attacks more biting. Ask her to work in this way until she is making really strong attacks. Suggest that when she makes an attack, she does so as if she really wants to believe it. And when she responds, urge her to really throw herself into it with the intention of demolishing the attack and of strengthening her conviction in her rational belief.

Remind your client that the purpose of this exercise is to strengthen her conviction in her rational belief, so it is important that she stops only when she has answered all of her attacks. If she makes an attack that she cannot respond to, suggest that she stop the exercise and raise the matter with you in her next session.

6 When your client has answered all of her attacks, ask her to re-rate her level of conviction in her rational belief using the 0%–100% scale as before. If your client has succeeded at responding persuasively to her attacks, then this rating will have gone up appreciably. If it has not increased or it has only done so a little, discuss this with her so that you can both discover what is preventing an increase in rational belief conviction.

Use rational-emotive imagery

Rational-emotive imagery (REI) is an imagery method designed to help your client to practise changing her *specific* irrational belief to its rational equivalent while simultaneously imagining what she is most disturbed about in the specific situation in question. Help your client to understand that this method will help her to strengthen her conviction in her new rational beliefs.

What follows is a set of instructions for using Albert Ellis's version of REI (Ellis & Maultsby, 1974).

INSTRUCTIONS FOR USING REI: ELLIS VERSION

1 Ask your client to take a situation in which she disturbed herself and then ask her to identify the aspect of the situation she was most disturbed about.
2 Ask your client to close her eyes and imagine the situation as vividly as possible and to focus on the adversity at 'A'.
3 Encourage your client to allow herself to experience fully the UNE that she felt at the time while still focusing intently on the 'A'. Ensure that your client's UNE is *one* of the following: anxiety, depression, shame, guilt, hurt, unhealthy anger, unhealthy jealousy, unhealthy envy.
4 Ask your client to really experience this disturbed emotion for a moment or two and then ask her to change her

emotional response to a HNE, while all the time focusing intently on the adversity at 'A'. Ask her not to change the intensity of the emotion, just the emotion itself. Thus, if her original UNE was anxiety, encourage her to change this to concern; if it was depression, have her change it to sadness. Ask her to change shame to disappointment, guilt to remorse, hurt to sorrow, unhealthy anger to healthy anger, unhealthy jealousy to healthy jealousy and unhealthy envy to healthy envy. Again ask her to change the UNE to its healthy equivalent, but to keep the level of intensity of the new emotion as strong as the old emotion. Suggest that she keep experiencing this new emotion for about 5 minutes, all the time focusing on the adversity at 'A'. If she goes back to the old UNE, ask her to bring the new HNE back.

5 At the end of 5 minutes, ask your client how she changed her emotion.

6 Make sure that your client changed her emotional response by changing her specific irrational belief to its healthy alternative. If she did not do so (if, for example, she changed her emotion by changing the 'A' to make it less negative or neutral or by holding an indifference belief about the 'A'), suggest that she does the exercise again and keep doing this until she has changed her emotion only by changing her specific unhealthy belief to its healthy alternative.

Encourage your client to practise REI several times a day and encourage her to aim for 30 minutes' daily practice when she is not doing any other therapy homework.

Suggest that your client rehearse her rational beliefs while acting in ways that are consistent with these beliefs

Perhaps the most powerful way of helping your client to strengthen her target rational belief is to encourage her to rehearse it while facing the relevant adversity at 'A' and while acting in ways that are consistent with this rational belief.

Thus, end a coaching session by negotiating a homework assignment that helps her to implement the above principle and is based on the work that you have already done in the session.

If you need to, help your client to see that when her behaviour and thinking are in sync and she keeps them in sync, she maximizes the chances of strengthening her conviction in her rational belief. Conversely, discourage her from acting and thinking in ways that are consistent with her old irrational belief.

Remember the following equation when negotiating a behavioural homework task with your client:

Face adversity at 'A' + Rehearse rB + Act in ways consistent with rB

Case study: Linda

I used all three techniques with Linda, which I will outline in Part 4.

Step 19: negotiate homework assignments

As a coach, you will be very familiar with the idea that your clients need to put into practice what they learn in coaching sessions if they are to realize their personal objectives. The same principle applies when you are helping a client to deal with her emotional problem so that she can resume working on her coaching goals. In RECBT the tasks that your client executes in the service of dealing effectively with her emotional problem are known as homework assignments. While they are traditionally negotiated at the end of coaching sessions, they can be agreed earlier. In which case, it is important to ensure that, at the end of the session, the client understands what she is going to do.

Principles in negotiating a homework assignment with your client

There are a number of important principles that it is important that you follow in negotiating a homework assignment with your client. I will briefly review them here.

Use a term for homework assignments that is acceptable to your client

While the generic term for a task that your client carries out between sessions is a homework assignment, some clients respond negatively to the term since it reminds them of school with its negative connotations. In such cases use a term that is more acceptable with your client.

Negotiate an assignment with your client. Do not assign it unilaterally

Coaching is an activity that is based on a collaborative relationship between coach and client. This is reflected in your stance towards homework assignments. It is important that you negotiate a homework assignment with your client, not assign one unilaterally.

Allow sufficient time in the session to negotiate the homework assignment properly

As you know, time is at a premium in coaching session and you will see from the previously discussed steps that you have much to do when helping your client address her emotional problem effectively. So, it is easy to get to the end of the session and realize that you have not negotiated a relevant homework assignment with your client. The best way to avoid this is to prioritize negotiating homework assignments in your mind and even have a visible prompt that you can consult in the session as a reminder. Allocating the last 10 minutes to such negotiation is a good rule of thumb.

Ensure that the homework assignment follows logically from the work you did with your client in the session

It is important that the assignment is relevant to the work that you have done in the session with your client and provides a good logical bridge between what you have discussed in the session and what your client has agreed to do between sessions.

Ensure that your client clearly understands the homework assignment

If the client does not understand what she has agreed to do, she is unlikely to do it.

Ensure that the homework assignment is relevant to your client dealing effectively with her emotional problem

If your client does not understand how the task she has agreed to do will help her to achieve her emotional goals and thus deal effectively with her emotional problem, she will be far less likely to do the task than if she has such understanding.

Ensure that the type of homework assignment you negotiated with your client is relevant to the stage reached by the two of you on her emotional problem

There are a number of different types of homework assignments and it is important that the type of assignment your client agrees to do is relevant to where you have got to in dealing with her emotional problem. Thus, a reading assignment is best suited to helping your client understand more about her emotional problem, a cognitive assignment best to give her practice at questioning her beliefs and a cognitive behavioural assignment best for helping her to act on her rational belief while simultaneously rehearsing it.

Employ the 'challenging, but not overwhelming' principle in negotiating the homework assignment

If you ask your client to do something that is too much for her then she will not do it. If you ask her to do something that is too easy for her then there is little therapeutic value to be gained for her. However, if you suggest that she does something that she can do, but will be difficult for her then she is likely both to do it and to gain from doing so.

Introduce and explain the 'no lose' concept of homework assignments

The 'no lose' concept in homework points to the fact that when your client does a homework assignment successfully, then she gains from doing so. However, if she fails to do it then this provides an opportunity to learn more about obstacles to change so that you can both effectively address such obstacles. The latter point should be particularly stressed when your client feels discouraged when she fails to do an assignment.

Ensure that your client has the necessary skills to carry out the homework assignment

If your client does not have the required skills to do her homework, then it is unlikely that she will do it or she will do it poorly. Thus, if Linda lacks the necessary assertive skills then she is unlikely to speak to her boss about his broken promise to her or she will do so poorly. Therefore, if your client lacks the necessary skills that a particular homework assignment calls for, teach her these skills before suggesting that she implements the assignment.

Ensure that your client thinks that she can do the homework assignment

Your client may have the required skills to do the assignment, but may think that she cannot do it. Encourage her to use imagery rehearsal in the session where she pictures herself successfully completing the assignment and to practise this technique between sessions before doing the task in actuality. Such imagery rehearsal is useful in helping your client see that she can do what she previously thought she could not do.

Elicit a firm commitment from your client that she will carry out the homework assignment

It is sometimes useful to ask your client to make a commitment to do a homework assignment. This may be with herself, with you or with a friend. If doing so increases the chances that your client will carry out the assignment then it is a useful technique.

Help your client to specify when, where and how often she will carry out the homework assignment

In this step-by-step guide, I have stressed the value of being specific as you assess your client's emotional problem and intervene accordingly. This principle is also useful in homework negotiation and if the assignment warrants it, then encourage your client to specify when, where and how often she is going to do the task. In my experience, encouraging your client to be specific reduces the chances that she will say that she did not do the assignment because she did not have time or opportunity to do so.

Help your client to rehearse the homework assignment in the session

If you have time to do so, then encouraging your client to rehearse the assignment in the coaching session can be valuable. Indeed, with some assignments such rehearsal is so important that I strongly urge you to devote time to it. Rehearsal may either be mental (where your client pictures herself carrying out the assignment in her mind's eye) or behavioural (where your client role-plays with you what she has agreed to do when that involves another person). In this latter case, you may need to know a little about the other person if you are to play the role of that person in a plausible manner. I played the role of Linda's boss when she rehearsed what she was going to say to him at her planned meeting.

It is important that you encourage your client to practise her rational belief before and during the rehearsal

Elicit from the client potential obstacles to homework completion and problem-solve these obstacles

The more you can encourage your client to identify potential obstacles to doing a negotiated homework assignment and either help them to circumvent such obstacles or to neutralize them, the more likely your client is to do the assignment. Unidentified obstacles will prevent your client from carrying out her homework assignment. Forewarned is forearmed for both of you.

Encourage your client and yourself to make and retain a written note of the homework assignment and its relevant details

Studies in medicine have shown that when the patient is given a written note by the physician of what medication to take, when and how often, then this increases patient compliance with the medication. This is useful in coaching too and I suggest that you encourage your client to make a written note of the assignment and related issues (e.g. time, place and frequency). It is important that you make a written note of this too in your notes. You may want to check that you both have an accurate record of the negotiated assignment if you suspect that this may not be the case.

Having discussed important issues with respect to homework negotiation, I will discuss similar issues with respect to reviewing homework in the following step.

Case study: Linda

I will discuss the homework assignments I negotiated with Linda in Part 4.

Step 20: review homework assignments

Negotiating suitable homework assignments with your client shows her that such assignments are an integral part of dealing with her emotional problem. However, you can undermine this if you fail to review them at the beginning of the following session. Unless there is a very good reason not to do so (e.g. your client is in a state of crisis) it is good coaching practice to review the assignment at the outset of the next session and to devote sufficient time to the review to underscore its importance.

Principles in reviewing a homework assignment with your client

When your client states that she did the homework assignment, check whether or not it was done as negotiated

When your client reports that she carried out the homework assignment, the first point to check when you review the homework assignment is whether or not she did it as negotiated. It may well be that your client changed the nature of the assignment and in doing so lessened the therapeutic potency of the assignment.

One common way in which your client may change the nature of her negotiated homework assignment is when she does not face the critical aspect of the situation that she has agreed to face. In RECBT parlance, she has not faced the 'A'. For example, let's suppose that your client has a fear of being rejected by a particular man. In the session you work carefully to identify, challenge and help her to change the irrational belief that underpins her anxiety. Following on from this work you negotiate with her an assignment that involves her practising her new rational belief in the face of actual rejection by the man. Because the client is afraid of rejection, it is important that she faces the prospect of rejection. At the next session, your client is pleased with the result of her homework. She asked the man if he wanted to go for a coffee and he accepted her invitation. However, you know that the client's 'A' was asking the man for a date.

As they are colleagues they often go for a coffee and the man would not have seen it as a 'date'. The important point to note from a therapeutic point of view is that the client has not faced the 'A' that she agreed to face i.e. the prospect of a date. She played safe.

How do you respond when it becomes clear that your client has changed the nature of her homework? I suggest that you do the following.

Step 1: Encourage your client by saying that you were pleased that she did the assignment.

Step 2: Explain how, in your opinion, she changed the assignment and remind her of the exact nature of the task as it was negotiated by the two of you in the previous session. In doing so, if indicated, remind your client of the purpose of the assignment, which dictated its precise form.

Step 3: If your client made a genuine mistake in changing the nature of the assignment, invite her to re-do the assignment, but this time as it was previously negotiated. If she agrees, ensure that she keeps a written reminder of the assignment and ask her to guard against making further changes to it. Don't forget to review the assignment in the following session. If she doesn't agree to do the assignment, explore and deal with this reluctance.

Step 4: If it appears that the change that your client made to the assignment was motivated by the presence of an implicit irrational belief, identify and deal with this belief and again invite your client to re-do the assignment as it was previously negotiated, urging her once again to guard against making further change to the assignment. Alternatively, modify the assignment in a way that takes into account the newly discovered obstacle.

Review what your client learned from doing the assignment

It is important that you ask your client what she learned from doing the homework. If your client learned what you hoped she would learn, acknowledge that she did well and move on. If your client did not learn what you hoped she would learn, then you need to address this issue. In particular, help her to learn the appropriate point and see if you can help her choose another assignment that will help her learn the point experientially and not just cognitively.

Capitalize on your client's success

When your client has successfully done her homework and has learned what you hoped she would learn, reinforce her for achievement and suggest that she builds on her success by perhaps choosing a more challenging assignment next time, if appropriate.

Responding to your client's homework 'failure'

Let us suppose that your client has done her homework, but it turned out poorly. When this happens, clients often say that they did the assignment, but 'it didn't work'. I have put the word 'failure' in inverted commas here because although clients regard the assignment as a 'failure', there is much to learn from this situation. So, when you encounter this so-called 'failure', remind your client of the 'no-lose' nature of homework assignments (discussed earlier) and begin to investigate the factors involved. But first ask for a factual account about what happened. Then, once you have identified the factors that accounted for the 'failure', help your client to deal with them and endeavour to renegotiate the same or a similar assignment. While you are investigating the factors which accounted for your client's homework 'failure', it is useful to keep in mind a number of such factors. Here is an illustrative list of some of the more common reasons for homework 'failure' and possible therapeutic responses.

- **Problem**: Your client implemented certain but not all the elements of the negotiated assignment. For example, your client may have done the behavioural aspect of the assignment, but did not practise new rational beliefs with the result that she experienced the same UNEs associated with the target problem.

Possible response: Suggest that she remember to rehearse her rational beliefs before the behavioural part of the task. Use an in-session imagery technique, if required.

- **Problem**: The assignment was 'overwhelming, rather than challenging' for your client at this time.
  Possible response: Encourage the client to see this as good feedback and recalibrate the assignment so that it is in the 'challenging' realm, not the 'overwhelming' realm.

- **Problem**: Your client began to do the assignment but stopped doing it because she began to experience discomfort which she believed she could not tolerate.
  Possible response: Help her to formulate an appropriate discomfort tolerance belief and suggest that she rehearses this next time this happens.

- **Problem**: Your client practised the wrong rational beliefs during the assignment.
  Possible response: Ascertain the reason for your client practising the wrong belief and suggest a suitable remedy. Suggest that she write the correct belief on a card and take it with her to review in relevant situations.

- **Problem**: Your client practised the right rational beliefs, but did so in an overly weak manner with the result that her UNEs predominated.
  Possible response: Suggest that she be more forceful with herself in rehearsing rational beliefs. Model this in the session, if necessary.

- **Problem**: Your client began to do the assignment, but forgot what she was to do after she had begun.
  Possible response: Suggest that she consults a written record of the assignment in such circumstances. If she 'forgets' to do so, the obstacle needs further assessment.

- **Problem**: Your client began the assignment, but gave up because she did not experience immediate benefit from it.
  Possible response: Help her to see that while such immediate benefit would be nice, it is not necessary and also not likely. Help her to take a longer-range view of such benefit.

- **Problem**: Your client began the assignment, but gave up soon after when she realized that she did not know what to do. This happens particularly with written 'ABC' homework assignments.

Possible response: Give her a set of written instructions concerning the task (see Dryden, 2001, for examples).

* **Problem**: Your client began the assignment, but encountered another 'A' that triggered a new undiscovered irrational belief which led her to abandon the assignment.

  Possible response: Suggest that if this happens again that she look for and challenge the new rational belief before returning to the agreed task.

Dealing with the situation when your client has not done the homework assignment

Despite the fact that you may have taken the utmost care in negotiating a homework assignment with your client and instituted all the safeguards that I discussed above, your client may still not carry it out. When this happens, I suggest that you follow a similar procedure that I previously discussed; that is, ask your client for a factual account of the situation where she contracted to do the assignment but did not do it, remind her of the 'no-lose' concept of homework assignments, identify and deal with the factors that accounted for her not doing the assignment and then renegotiate the same or a similar assignment. As you investigate the aforementioned factors, be particularly aware of the fact that you may have failed to institute one or more of the safeguards reviewed above. If this is the case and your failure to do so accounts for your client not carrying out the assignment, then take responsibility for this omission, disclose this to your client, institute the safeguard and renegotiate the assignment.

On the other hand, if the reason why your client did not do the assignment can be attributed to a factor in the client that you could not have foreseen, help her to deal with it and again renegotiate the same or a similar assignment.

Case study: Linda

I will discuss my review of Linda's homework assignments in Part 4.

Step 21: revisit and question 'A' if necessary

In Step 8 (pp. 84–87), when I discussed identifying your client's 'A', I urged you to encourage your client to assume temporarily that her 'A' (i.e. the aspect of the situation that she was most disturbed about in the situation under consideration) was true. This 'A' is her individualistic adversity. I explained that you need to do this because this is the best way for you to identify the unhealthy irrational beliefs that lie at the core of your client's disturbed reactions at 'C' in the ABC framework. If you were to question your client's 'A' earlier in the emotional episode under consideration because you thought it was obviously distorted, you may help your client to realize this and she may feel better as a result. However, she would not have gained practice at identifying, challenging and changing her irrational beliefs that according to RECBT theory lie at the core of your client's emotional problem. Consequently, these beliefs would remain intact and would be triggered the next time she reviews examples of her problem in her mind or encounters the same 'A' in related situations.

In addition, because your client's disturbed feelings stem largely from her irrational belief about 'A' rather than from 'A' itself, your attempts to help your client to question this 'A' while she holds an irrational belief about it will be coloured by this belief and any reconsideration of the distorted inference she may have made at 'A' will probably be short-lived. Alternatively, once she has made progress at changing her irrational belief about 'A', she is more likely to be in a more objective frame of mind and it is this frame of mind that best facilitates her questioning of 'A'.

You may not need to help your client to question 'A' if it is clear that she is not distorted when saying that it represents an individualistic adversity. Thus, when Linda claims that her boss broke his promise to promote her, she provided evidence that supported this inference. As such, there is no point in revisiting 'A'. You only need to revisit 'A' when it seems as if it may be distorted and your client has not corrected the distorted inference herself after Step 17 which is when I suggest that you revisit and question 'A' if you need to.

How to question 'A'

So how do you go about helping your client to question 'A'? By going back to it and asking her whether or not this was the most realistic way of looking at the situation. This does not mean that she can know for certain that her 'A' was true or false for there is rarely any absolute and agreed correct way of viewing an event. What it does mean is that your client can weigh up all the evidence that is available to her about the situation at hand and make what is likely to be the 'best bet' about what happened.

I now list a number of ways that you can help your client question 'A' so that she can determine whether or not it was the most realistic way of viewing what happened in the situation in which she disturbed yourself. In doing so I will show how I helped Harriet, another one of my coaching clients, question her 'A', after she made progress developing her rational belief about this 'A'. Harriet's 'A' was that she thought that she was about to be sacked from her job because her boss was critical of a report that she had written. She was very anxious about this at 'C' and could not concentrate on the personal objectives she had set in coaching. As I said, she had made good strides at dealing with her anxiety after I had encouraged her to assume that she was about to be sacked.

1 Encourage your client to go back to her ABC and focus on what she wrote under the heading 'situation'. Then, ask her whether what she listed under 'A' was the most realistic way of viewing the situation given all the evidence to hand. This involves her considering the inference that she made that formed 'A', considering alternative inferences, evaluating all the possibilities and choosing the most realistic inference

   • Harriet asked herself how likely it was that she would be sacked just after her boss had been critical of her report. In formulating an answer to this question, Harriet considered the following.

   i   Has my boss been critical of the work of others

and they have not been subsequently fired from their job?

Answer: No. My boss has very exacting standards and he is critical of people's work when they have not met those standards. But, in the last year only one person has been fired for poor work and this was only after he received verbal and written warnings about the quality of his work.

ii Have I received any such warnings?

Answer: No.

iii What has been the reaction of my boss to my other work?

Answer: It has generally been good. This is the first time he has criticized my work. Before he has said that I have done a good job or he has said nothing at all.

- Harriet identified alternative explanations for and implications of her boss's criticism and came up with the following.

i My report was not up to standard and my boss was correct to criticize me, but he was not going to fire me or issue any warning.

ii My report was not up to standard and my boss was correct to criticize me and he was not going to fire me, but he would issue a verbal warning.

iii My report was up to standard, but my boss criticized it because he was in a bad mood about something else.

- Finally, Harriet reviewed the evidence concerning the likelihood of these alternative explanations. In doing so, she took into account what she knew about her boss (i.e. he was not a man to allow his moods to colour his feedback to staff) and the level of her own work.
- After she answered her own questions and reviewed the other alternative explanations for her boss's behaviour Harriet concluded, based on the evidence at hand, that her report was not up to standard, but that her boss would neither fire her nor issue a verbal warning to her.

However, what if Harriet's boss had indicated before that he was unhappy with Harriet's work and had issued both a verbal and a written warning to her about the quality of her work? If this was the case when Harriet came to question her 'A', she would be likely to decide that her 'A' was the best bet of all the inferences she had identified (i.e. the fact that her boss criticized her work meant that she was about to be fired). However, it could still have turned out that her boss would not have fired her. Consequently, it is important to keep in mind that even your client's best bet at 'A' may prove to be wrong.

2 Other questions that you can ask your client about 'A' are as follows.

- How likely is it that 'A' happened (or might happen)?
- Would an objective jury agree that 'A' happened or might happen? If not, what would the jury's verdict be?
- Did you view (are you viewing) the situation realistically? If not, how could you have viewed (can you view) it more realistically?
- If you asked someone whom you could trust to give you an objective opinion about the truth or falsity of your inference about the situation at hand, what would the person say to you and why? How would this person encourage you to view the situation instead?
- If a friend had told you that they had faced (were facing or were about to face) the same situation as you faced and had made the same inference, what would you say to him/her about the validity of their inference and why? How would you encourage the person to view the situation instead?

Part 4

Case study: Linda

In this part of the book I will bring together the various excerpts of the work I did with Linda that I used to illustrate many of the points I discussed in the step-by step guide. I am doing this to give you a flavour of how such work flows and unfolds over time. Please refer to the appropriate step in the step-by-step guide for further information on the presented issues.

I was coaching Linda who was not feeling challenged in life. In our first two coaching sessions I established where she needed to be challenged in life and we set a number of goals that she agreed to pursue before the next coaching session. Before I saw her next she learned that she failed to get promotion that had been promised to her by her boss. In presenting relevant dialogue, I will sometimes comment on my thinking as a coach and connect this with how I intervened with Linda. I will do this to help you understand the reasons for my interventions with Linda.

Step 1: determining whether or not Linda has an emotional problem. If she has, determining whether or not she is stuck and whether or not she can bypass it to pursue her personal objectives

Here is how I helped Linda and myself determine whether or not she had a problem about failing to be promoted.

Does Linda have an emotional problem?

WINDY: Since we last met what have you done to pursue your wish to get more challenge into your life?

LINDA: Well, I felt really inspired at the end of the last session. However, a few days later I found out from my boss that he was not going to promote me even though he had promised that he would do so.

WINDY: And how do you feel about this?

LINDA: Well, I felt and still feel really upset about it.

[Windy's observation: The term 'upset' is too vague for me to determine what type of emotion Linda is feeling and whether her emotional response is unhealthy or healthy. So I need to clarify this. I will do this by using her term 'upset' but linking it with more specific negative emotions.]

WINDY: Do you feel hurt upset, angry upset or . . .?

LINDA: Angry upset definitely.

[Windy's observation: OK, so now I know that Linda is angry, but I now need to find out whether this anger is healthy or not. I will start by looking at her behaviour.]

WINDY: When you feel angry how to do express it?

LINDA: I don't.

[Windy's observation: Having drawn a blank here, I will now assess her action tendency which is how she feels like expressing her anger but doesn't act on this feeling.]

WINDY: When you feel angry what do you feel like doing, but suppress?

LINDA: I feel like ripping him to shreds and giving him a real piece of my mind.

[Windy's observation: This seems very much like problematic or unhealthy anger, but I will double check by assessing her associated thinking.]

WINDY: And how much do you think about this?

LINDA: It keeps going round and round in my mind. I can't seem to concentrate on anything else. So although I was planning to do a lot of preparatory work for this session, I just haven't had the mental space to do any.

[Windy's observation: Since angry rumination is a feature of unhealthy anger this seems to confirm my hunch that Linda's anger is problematic for her. I will now ask her directly about this.]

WINDY: It's understandable that you feel angry about this, but anger can be healthy or unhealthy. While you don't express how you feel directly, you say that you feel like giving your boss a piece of your mind and ripping him to shreds. You also say that you are ruminating about this event a lot. Standing back for a moment, do you think that your anger is healthy or unhealthy?

LINDA: Put like that, I think it's really unhealthy.

Having ascertained that Linda does have another emotional problem, I proceed as follows.

Is Linda stuck?

WINDY: What have you tried to do to help yourself deal with your anger?

LINDA: Well, I have discussed what happened with my partner and friends, but they just seem to think that my anger is justified. My partner wants to confront my boss and 'punch his lights out'. I have tried punching a cushion and doing relaxation exercises, but nothing seems to help apart from in the very short term.

[Windy's observation: It seems that nothing Linda has tried has helped her to deal with her problematic anger. Let's see if she has any plans to deal with it more effectively.]

WINDY: Do you have any plans to deal with your anger?
LINDA: I was hoping that you might be able to help me in this respect.

[Windy's observation: Sounds like a specific invitation for me to intervene. But first, I want to double check to see if Linda's anger is an obstacle to her pursuing her personal objectives.]

Having ascertained that Linda is bogged down with her emotional problem, I proceed as follows.

Is Linda's emotional problem an obstacle to her pursuing her personal objectives?

WINDY: You said earlier that after our last session you felt inspired to put into practice what we discussed. Then, a few days later you found out that you were not going to get the promotion you were promised. Now, we have established that you feel unhealthily angry about this and we know that you feel stuck with your angry feelings. Is that right?
LINDA: That's correct.

> *[Windy's observation: Now I need to establish whether or not Linda is able to compartmentalize this problem and keep working towards her personal objectives.]*
>
> WINDY: Have you been able to 'park' your angry feelings and keep working towards your personal objectives or have they gotten in the way of you doing so?
>
> LINDA: To be honest with you, I have let our work go because my mind has been on the promotion issue.
>
> *[Windy's observation: Finally, I'm going to assess whether or not Linda will be able to compartmentalize her angry feelings in the future.]*
>
> WINDY: And do you think that on your own you will be able to 'park' these feelings in the future and concentrate on our work together or do you think you might want some help to deal with your unhealthy feelings?
>
> LINDA: I don't think that I would know how to 'park' these feelings as you call it. I would value some help.

Having established that Linda had an emotional problem, was bogged down with it and could not compartmentalize it, I discussed with her how we might deal with this.

Discussing how we might deal with Linda's emotional problem

> WINDY: OK, now there are a couple of possibilities here. First, I could help you with this emotional problem myself. This would involve me assuming temporarily a counselling role. Because it is temporary, doing so is not incompatible with my

work as a coach. Second, I could refer you to a counselling colleague who will help you with this and when you are ready, we could resume our coaching work. What's your view?

LINDA: Well, if you can help me with this. I would like you to help me with the problem.

Step 2: eliciting Linda's explicit agreement to target this emotional problem for change and establishing a contingency plan if I fail to help her

Eliciting an agreement to target Linda's emotional problem for change

> *WINDY:* So, Linda, let me summarize where we have got to so far. OK?
>
> *LINDA:* OK.
>
> *WINDY:* In our coaching work, we had identified your wish to be challenged more in life and you had been quite excited about beginning to identify how you might go about seeking such challenges. Then, your boss, who had promised to promote you, didn't do so. You responded with anger and we established that this anger is problematic in the sense that you have become stuck in your angry feelings and can't 'park' it sufficiently to keep focused on your coaching objective. Is this accurate?
>
> *LINDA:* Very.
>
> *WINDY:* We further considered how we were going to deal with this obstacle and we agreed that I was going to help you deal with this obstacle myself. Is that your understanding?
>
> *LINDA:* Yes it is.

Establishing a contingency plan

> *WINDY:* OK. Before we start, let's consider what happens if I can't help you with this obstacle. OK?
>
> *LINDA:* OK.
>
> *WINDY:* We need to establish a contingency plan to deal

with this situation. I suggest that if this happens that I refer you to one of my colleagues who is a counsellor and who would work with you more intensively to deal with this emotional problem. Then, when you are ready, we would resume our coaching work. How does that sound?

LINDA: Sounds good.

WINDY: OK, so let's go forward on that basis. OK?

LINDA: OK.

Step 3: formulating the problem that is serving as an obstacle to Linda's pursuit of her personal objectives

> *WINDY:* Now we are focusing on your emotional problem, let me just review what you told me when we first talked about it. OK?
>
> *LINDA:* OK.
>
> *WINDY:* Well, you made yourself angry about your boss not promoting you after telling you that he would. We discovered that your anger was unhealthy because you felt like ripping him to shreds and you were ruminating about the situation. Is that correct?
>
> *LINDA:* Yes, it is.

Formalizing Linda's formulated problem

> 1 Situation: *My boss told me that I would get promotion, but then he did not promote me.*
> 2 'A': *Not known yet.*
> 3 'C' (emotional): *Unhealthy anger.*
> 4 'C' (behavioural): *Felt like ripping my boss to shreds.*
> 5 'C' (cognitive): *Ruminating about not being promoted and what I would like to do to my boss.*
> 6 Effect on coaching goals: *This is stopping me from concentrating on and pursuing my coaching goals.*

Putting this into a sentence we have Linda's formulated problem.

> *My boss told me that I would get promotion, but then he did not promote me. I feel unhealthily angry about this and feel*

like ripping my boss to shreds. I ruminate about doing so and about not being promoted. This is stopping me from concentrating on and pursuing my coaching goals.

Step 4: setting a goal with respect to the formulated problem

WINDY: OK, Linda, let's see how you would like to handle the situation of being passed over for promotion by your boss. OK?

LINDA: OK.

WINDY: Well, we know that this situation happened so we can't do anything to prevent it from happening. Right?

LINDA: Well, I hope to get him to change his mind.

WINDY: Indeed, but you can't undo the past can you?

LINDA: Sadly, no.

WINDY: You mentioned you hope to get your boss to change his mind. Will your unhealthy anger and suppressing your wish to tear him to shreds help you to do this?

[Windy's observation: Here I am preparing the ground for setting goals by encouraging Linda to see the link between her unhealthy anger and her preferred outcome.]

LINDA: No, it won't.

WINDY: So would you be interested in a way of responding that reflects the negativity of your boss not keeping his promise to promote, but enables you to assert yourself with him and also to resume your work towards your coaching goals without being preoccupied with the situation?

[Windy's observation: Here, I am suggesting that Linda considers a goal comprising what in RECBT we call a healthy negative emotion and related behavioural and cognitive responses.]

LINDA: That sounds good.

WINDY: So I could help you feel healthily angry rather than unhealthily angry about your boss not promoting you. This would lead you to be assertive with him rather than wanting to rip him to shreds. Also, it would help you to get on with things with this in the back of your mind rather than ruminating on it. How does that sound?

[Windy's observation: In this intervention, I am explicitly contrasting unhealthy anger with healthy anger and their respective behavioural and cognitive responses.]

LINDA: Well, if you can help me do that, it would be great.

Formalizing Linda's goals with respect to her formulated problem

Here, more formally, are the goals set by Linda whose emotional problem was formulated in Step 3. As noted above, the first two points are the same in the goal section as in the formulated problem section.

1 Situation: *My boss told me that I would get promotion, but then he did not promote me.*
2 'A': *Not known yet.*
3 'C' (emotional goal): *Healthy anger (rather than unhealthy anger).*
4 'C' (behavioural): *Telling my boss that I was annoyed about this and asking him to explain his decision (rather than wanting to rip him to shreds).*
5 'C' (cognitive): *Being aware of his decision, but getting on with things (rather than ruminating about it).*
6 Effect on coaching goals: *Being able to concentrate on and pursue my coaching goals.*

Putting this into a sentence we have the client's goal with respect to her formulated target problem:

My boss told me that I would get promotion, but then he did not promote me. I want to feel healthy anger (rather than unhealthy anger) about this and to tell him that I was annoyed about this and then ask him to explain his decision (rather than wanting to rip him to shreds). I want to be aware of his decision, but get on with things (rather than ruminating about it). Doing this will help me to concentrate on and pursue my coaching goals.

Step 5: assessing for the presence of a meta-emotional problem and deciding with Linda if this is to become the target problem

Here is how I addressed this issue with Linda.

WINDY: OK. So you can see that your anger is unhealthy. Can you also see that healthy anger, where you feel like asserting yourself and in fact do assert yourself with your boss, and where you get on with life, mindful of the incident, but without rumination is constructive?

LINDA: Yes.

WINDY: Before we get down to the business of helping you, I just want to bring up one issue. Now, when you make yourself unhealthily angry and you focus on that anger how do you feel about your angry feelings?

LINDA: Well . . . I'm not sure what you mean.

WINDY: OK. For example, do you feel ashamed of feeling that way, or anxious . . .?

LINDA: Oh, I see. No. I am too busy feeling angry . . .

WINDY: What about when you calm down and focus on your anger then?

[Windy's observation: This is an important point. Your client may disturb themselves about their unhealthy negative emotion (UNE) either at the time or later when they are not in the grip of such feelings. It is worth asking about both possibilities.]

LINDA: No, if anything I feel justified in how I feel . . . But, now I can see that there is the possibility of feeling and reacting with healthy anger, I guess I can feel justified in feeling anger and still be healthy.

[Windy's observation: Linda raises a number of important points here. First, your client may well construe their UNE

positively and this needs to be tackled if it persists later in the process. Second, your client may change their mind about the perceived benefit of her UNE when she understands and commits herself to the healthy alternative to this UNE, i.e. her healthy negative emotion (HNE).]

WINDY: Good point. So as you don't have what we call a meta-emotional problem, literally an emotional problem about your unhealthy anger, we can proceed to helping you deal with your unhealthy anger.

Step 6: asking for a concrete example of Linda's formulated target problem

> WINDY: So now let's discuss your unhealthy anger. It would be useful if you could pick a specific example of your anger problem with your boss. This might be something that has happened, is happening or you anticipate happening.
>
> LINDA: Well, I would like to talk to him about it, but I think if I do I will lose my temper.
>
> WINDY: So, let's focus on that. Can you tell me about the specific situation you envisage?
>
> *[Windy's observation: As Linda has chosen a future specific example, I need to get as much detail as I can about this likely context.]*
>
> LINDA: Well, it would be in his office just before lunch and I would have asked to see him about not being promoted.
>
> *[Windy's observation: This is sufficient detail to go on to the next step.]*

Step 7: identifying 'C'

As you will see from the above, when I asked Linda for a specific example of her anger problem she chose a future example where she would be in her boss's office just before lunch having asked to see him about not being promoted. This is how I identified her emotional 'C' in this situation.

WINDY: So how do you think you will feel in your boss's office just before lunch having asked to see him about not being promoted?

LINDA: I would feel angry.

[Windy's observation: Although Linda's formulated problem is unhealthy anger, I am not going to assume that her anger in the specific example she has chosen is necessarily unhealthy. I need to get evidence before concluding that it is and helping Linda to see this.]

WINDY: Your anger could be healthy or unhealthy and I would like to clarify which it is if that is OK?

LINDA: That's fine.

WINDY: When you anticipate feeling angry what would you feel like doing at that moment?

LINDA: I wouldn't do this, of course, but I would feel like shouting abuse at him and giving him a slap.

WINDY: Now does that sound like healthy anger to you?

LINDA (laughing): Certainly not!

Step 8: identifying 'A'

Here is how I actually identified Linda's 'A'.

WINDY: So what do you think you would be most angry about when you went to see your boss to discuss not being promoted?

LINDA: Well, he said he would promote me and then he didn't do so.

WINDY: So apart from giving you promotion, what could you learn about at the meeting that would eliminate or significantly reduce your unhealthy anger?

[Windy's observation: This is a version of 'Windy's magic question' technique explained on pp. 84–85]

LINDA: Well, I am pretty sure that he will try to wriggle out of it, but I think that if he convinced me that he hadn't broken his promise to me, then that would definitely help.

WINDY: So would I be correct in assuming, then, that you would be most unhealthily angry about your boss breaking his promise to you and not promoting you when he said he would?

LINDA: Absolutely. I really do have a thing about broken promises.

Step 9: eliciting Linda's emotional goal in the specific example being assessed

WINDY: So, instead of feeling unhealthily angry and feeling like shouting abuse at him and giving him a slap, what is your goal in this situation?

LINDA: To get him to change his mind.

[Windy's observation: Linda is focused on changing her boss rather than changing her responses, so let me address this issue.]

WINDY: Who is ultimately in charge of your boss's decision to promote you: him or you?

LINDA: Sadly, him.

WINDY: What are you in charge of with respect to, as you put it, 'getting him to change his mind'?

LINDA: I guess my own behaviour.

WINDY: You guessed right! . . . (both laugh) . . . So is feeling like shouting abuse at him and giving him a slap a good foundation for increasing the chances of influencing him to promote you?

LINDA (laughs): No.

WINDY: And what alternative behaviour would increase your chances?

LINDA: Being assertive with him and coming up with rational arguments as to why he should keep his promise to promote me.

WINDY: And will your feelings of unhealthy anger help you or hinder you in this respect?

LINDA: It will hinder me . . . definitely.

WINDY: So you need a feeling that acknowledges the badness of your boss's broken promise to you and that helps you to assert yourself and give those rational arguments. Would you want to set that as your feeling goal?

LINDA: Sounds good.

WINDY: So what would you call that emotion? Remember it needs to be negative and acknowledges the badness of the broken promise, but it also needs to help you to be assertive and give rational arguments.

LINDA: I would like to call it being constructively annoyed.

WINDY: Rather than unhealthily angry?

LINDA: Yes.

[Windy's observation: It is important to use a client's language when referring to a healthy negative emotion goal. Constructive annoyance is close enough to healthy anger to be acceptable, in my view.]

WINDY: So let me sum up. Rather than feel unhealthily angry with your boss for breaking his promise to you, you have set as your goal to feel constructively annoyed about the broken promise instead. While unhealthy anger leads you to want to shout abuse at your boss and slap him, an urge which fortunately you are able to suppress, constructive annoyance would help to actually assert yourself with him and allow you to provide rational arguments why he should change his mind back and keep his promise. However, you also recognize that all you can do is to control your own behaviour and you recognize that no matter how persuasive you may be, in the final analysis your boss is in charge of whether or not he chooses to promote you. Is that summary accurate?

LINDA: Very accurate.

Step 10: helping Linda to understand the 'B'–'C' connection

Asking Linda whether 'C' is determined by 'A' or by 'B'

> WINDY: So, Linda, we now know that you feel unhealthily angry towards your boss for breaking his promise towards you by not promoting you. Right?
>
> LINDA: Right.
>
> WINDY: But what largely determines your unhealthy anger, his broken promise or your belief about his broken promise?
>
> LINDA: Well, I'm tempted to say his broken promise because then I can blame him, but if I am honest, I guess it's my belief about his broken promise.

Step 11: identifying 'iBs', teaching 'rBs' and making the appropriate connections with 'C'

Using the theory-driven choice enquiry approach with Linda; 1: demand and non-dogmatic preference

WINDY: OK, Linda, I want to see if I can understand and help you to understand the belief that accounts for your unhealthy anger about your boss's broken promise to you. Now we know it was important to you that he did not break his promise. Correct?

LINDA: Correct.

WINDY: Now, given that, your belief could go one of two ways. I want to put these two beliefs to you so that you can tell which belief would underpin your unhealthy anger when you see your boss. OK?

LINDA: OK.

WINDY: Good, Here's belief Number 1: 'It's important to me that my boss not break his promise to promote me and therefore he absolutely should not have done so'. Now here is belief Number 2: 'It's important to me that my boss not break his promise to promote me, but sadly and regretfully he does not have to do what I want him to do'.

   Which belief would underpin your unhealthy anger at the time when you experience it?

LINDA: Belief Number 1.

WINDY: And which belief would lead you to feel constructively annoyed about the broken promise rather than unhealthy anger?

LINDA: Belief Number 2.

Using the theory-driven choice enquiry
approach with Linda; 2: other-depreciation and
other-acceptance beliefs

> WINDY: OK, Linda, now as you anticipate feeling
> unhealthy anger towards your boss for break-
> ing his promise to support you, I want to see if I
> can understand and help you to understand the
> belief towards your boss that stems from your
> demand and accounts for your unhealthy anger
> towards him. Now we know that you think that
> it is bad that your boss broke his promise to
> promote you, but when you are unhealthily
> angry, do you believe that he is bad for acting
> badly or do you believe that he is not bad, but a
> fallible human being for acting badly?
>
> LINDA: I believe he is bad.
>
> WINDY: And how would you feel if you believe that
> he is not bad, but a fallible human being for
> acting badly?
>
> LINDA: Constructively annoyed.

Now that I have helped Linda to see the link between her
irrational beliefs (demand and other-depreciation belief)
and her unhealthy anger, on the one hand and the link
between her rational belief (non-dogmatic preference and
other-acceptance belief) and her constructive annoyance,
on the other, she is ready to make a commitment to pursue her emotional and/or behavioural goals and to see that
changing her irrational beliefs is the best way of doing
this. In the next step, I will show how you can elicit this
commitment.

**Step 12: eliciting commitment from Linda to pursue
her emotional and/or behavioural goals and helping
her to see that changing her irrational beliefs is the
best way of doing this**

WINDY: OK, Linda, so you can see that your demand
and other-depreciation belief underpins your
unhealthy anger towards your boss and that
your non-dogmatic preference and your other-
acceptance belief underpins your feelings of
constructive annoyance. So if you want to feel
constructively annoyed instead of unhealthily
angry towards your boss what do you need to
change?

LINDA: My irrational beliefs.

WINDY: Would you like to make a commitment to doing
this or do you have some doubts or reservations
about doing so?

LINDA: Well, I have one reservation.

WINDY: What's that?

LINDA: If I am constructively annoyed then my feelings
will be light and won't reflect the badness of
what my boss did to me.

*[Windy's observation: This is a common misconception
about healthy negative feelings that clients have. In reality, because rational beliefs can be strongly held and
reflect the importance of what your client wants, but
does not demand, a healthy negative emotion can vary in
intensity according to this level of importance. Thus, constructive annoyance can be mild, moderate or strong
depending upon how important your client's non-
dogmatic preference is.]*

WINDY: Not necessarily. For example, if your rational
belief is as follows: 'I mildly want my boss to
keep his promise, but he does not have to do
so', then the intensity of your constructive

annoyance will be mild or light if he breaks his promise. If your belief is: 'I moderately want my boss to keep his promise, but he does not have to do so', then your constructive annoyance will be moderate if he breaks his promise. And finally, if your belief is: 'I very strongly want my boss to keep his promise, but he still does not have to do so', then your constructive annoyance is very strong when your boss breaks his promise. So, you see, your constructive annoyance can reflect the badness of what your boss did as long as your non-dogmatic preference is strong. Does that answer your reservation?

LINDA: Very much so.

Step 13: questioning both irrational and rational beliefs: choosing a strategy

As I had used assessment techniques that required Linda to compare and contrast her irrational belief with her rational belief alternative and she seemed to find this helpful, I decided to use a questioning strategy where I questioned her relevant irrational and rational beliefs together.

Step 14: questioning a demand and a non-dogmatic preference

WINDY: OK, Linda, let's begin questioning your beliefs, by looking at your demand and non-dogmatic preference which I am going to write up on the whiteboard.

I then write up the following:

Demand: It's important to me that my boss not break his promise to promote me . . . and therefore he absolutely should not have done so.

Non-dogmatic preference: It's important to me that my boss not break his promise to promote me . . . but sadly and regretfully he does not have to do what I want him to do.

WINDY: Now if you look at these two beliefs, which is true and which is false?

LINDA: My demand is false and my non-dogmatic preference is true.

WINDY: Why is that?

LINDA: Well, it's true that I want my boss not to break his promise, but it's not true that he must do what I want him to do.

WINDY: Why not?

LINDA: Because he is in charge of his decisions and I am not.

WINDY: Is that a persuasive argument for you?

[Windy's observation: In my view it is important that a client develops persuasive arguments in favour of her rational beliefs and against her irrational beliefs.]

LINDA: Well, yes, I was brought up to think that people in authority were honourable and kept their promises. I now see that this is true for some people, but not all. And my boss does not have to be the way I want him to be in this respect. He is the way he is. So that is a good argument.

WINDY: OK. Now which of these two beliefs is sensible and which is not?

LINDA: Again my non-dogmatic preference is sensible and my demand is not.

WINDY: Why?

LINDA: Because there is no logical connection between what I want and what has to be.

WINDY: Is that persuasive?

LINDA: Kind of, but not as persuasive as the idea that my boss does not have to be the way I want him to be. He is the way he is.

WINDY: OK, now which of these beliefs is healthier for you and which is less healthy?

LINDA: My non-dogmatic preference is better for me in all sorts of ways.

WINDY: Can you name a few?

LINDA: Well, it will help me to be relatively calm when I talk to him. It will help me to adjust constructively if I can't get him to change his mind and promote me and it will help me to concentrate on other things.

WINDY: Whereas your demand?

LINDA: Well, it gives me the results I have already discussed with you. I feel like exploding with him, which isn't good if I am going to have a meeting with him. It leads to rumination and I can't concentrate on my coaching work with you.

WINDY: Is that a persuasive argument?

LINDA: Very!

WINDY: So I suggest that you make a note of those two persuasive arguments.

LINDA: OK.

WINDY: Finally, which of these two beliefs do you want to commit to strengthening?

LINDA: My non-dogmatic preference.

WINDY: Do you have any reservations about giving up your demand?

[Windy's observation: Sometimes clients have doubts, reservations and objections to changing their irrational beliefs. It is best to know about them so you can respond to them. If your client harbours any such doubts, for example, and you don't know about them they will interfere with your client changing her irrational beliefs.]

LINDA: Well, when I think that he must keep his promise, I hold on to a view of the world where fairness triumphs in the end and it's tough giving that up.

WINDY: Do you think that holding that belief makes fairness triumph in the end?

LINDA: Sadly, no.

WINDY: Does acknowledging that help?

LINDA: Well, it's like swallowing a bitter pill. It will do you good, but it doesn't taste nice.

WINDY: So is it worth it to swallow the bitter pill and commit yourself to your non-dogmatic preference?

LINDA: Yes, it is.

Step 15: questioning an awfulizing and a non-awfulizing belief

As Linda selected her other-depreciation belief as the irrational belief stemming from her demand that best accounted for her unhealthy anger, I did not question her awfulizing belief and alternative non-awfulizing belief.

Step 16: questioning a discomfort intolerance belief and a discomfort tolerance belief

As Linda selected her other-depreciation belief as the irrational belief stemming from her demand that best accounted for her unhealthy anger, I did not question her discomfort intolerance and alternative discomfort tolerance belief.

Step 17: questioning a depreciation belief and an acceptance belief

WINDY: OK, Linda, let's continue by questioning your other-depreciation and other-acceptance beliefs, which again I am going to write up on the whiteboard.

I then write up the following:

Other-depreciation belief: It is bad that my boss broke his promise to promote me and therefore he is bad for doing so.

Other-acceptance belief: It is bad that my boss broke his promise to promote me, but he is not bad for doing so. He is a fallible human being who acted badly.

WINDY: Now which of these two beliefs is true and which is false?

LINDA: Well, when I'm really angry the other-depreciation belief feels true, but I know it's not.

WINDY: Why not?

LINDA: Well, doing something bad does not make my boss a bad person.

WINDY: Why not?

LINDA: Because he is ordinary and fallible. If he was bad he would be incapable of doing good and I know that's not true.

WINDY: How do you know that?

LINDA: Because he has done good things for me before and for others too. I know his family love him and he is always showing concern for his aged mum. So there is a lot of good about him.

WINDY: As well as bad?

LINDA: As well as bad.

WINDY: Do you find any of these arguments persuasive?

LINDA: The idea that he is a complicated mixture of

good and bad, rather than all bad is particularly persuasive.

WINDY: OK, now, as you look at the two beliefs on the board which is sensible and which is not?

LINDA: The other-acceptance is sensible and the other one isn't?

WINDY: Why is that?

LINDA: Because when I hold the other-depreciation belief, I think that his bad behaviour towards me when he broke his promise defines him as a person whereas when I hold the other one I don't think that?

WINDY: Is that a persuasive argument?

LINDA: Yes it is.

WINDY: Now when you look at the two beliefs again which is healthy for you and which isn't?

LINDA: For the same reasons as with my demand and non-dogmatic preference, my other-depreciation belief is unhealthy as it leads to explosive anger feelings, rumination and I can't get on with anything. I feel my life is on hold. My other-acceptance belief, on the other hand, leads me to feel annoyed, but in a constructive way so that I can talk to my boss. Also, it helps me to think about other things and get on with my life.

WINDY: And which of these two beliefs do you want to commit to strengthening?

LINDA: My other-acceptance belief.

WINDY: Do you have any reservations about giving up the other-depreciation belief?

LINDA: Well, that belief makes me feel powerful at the time, but that's a momentary thing. So no, not really.

Step 18: helping Linda to strengthen her conviction in her rational beliefs and weaken her conviction in her irrational beliefs

In order to help Linda to strengthen her conviction in her rational belief and weaken her conviction in her irrational belief, I employed three techniques: (1) the attack-response technique, (2) rational-emotive imagery, and (3) a behaviourally based technique where she rehearsed her rational belief and acted in a way that was consistent with this belief in a relevant situation. I have described these techniques in general in Step 18 of the step-by-step guide in Part 3 of this book (pp. 144–149).

Teaching Linda the attack-response technique

In helping Linda strengthen her conviction in her rational beliefs, I first taught her the attack-response technique (see pp. 145–147) and suggested that she did it for homework. I will discuss what she did and how I responded in the section on reviewing homework.

Teaching Linda rational-emotive imagery

I then taught Linda rational-emotive imagery (see pp. 147–148). I asked her to close her eyes and imagine that when she goes into her meeting with her boss, she focuses on him breaking his promise to promote her. I then encouraged her to make herself unhealthily angry about this; which she found quite easy to do as you might imagine. Then, while still focusing on the broken promise, I asked her to make herself constructively annoyed about this rather than unhealthily angry. When she did this, I asked how she effected the change and after a few times when she gave me a benign interpretation of his behaviour (e.g. 'It wasn't his fault, it was his superiors'), she effected the change by changing her belief to: 'He was wrong to break his promise to me, but he does not have to do the right thing. He is fallible, not bad for doing the wrong thing'. Once she understood how to change her feelings by changing her belief, I suggested that she practise this several times a day.

Linda rehearses her rational beliefs while acting in ways that are consistent with these beliefs

Perhaps the most powerful way that Linda could strengthen her conviction in her rational belief was to act in ways that are consistent with this belief. The main way in which Linda did this was to talk to her boss about feelings of constructive annoyance about him breaking his promise to promote her. Before she did this, she rehearsed her rational belief that she put into her words (i.e. 'My boss is not bad for breaking his promise to promote me. He is fallible and does not have to keep his promise.') and she kept this is mind while she talked to him. I will discuss what happened in the section on reviewing homework assignments below.

Step 19: negotiating homework assignments

I negotiated a number of homework assignments with Linda that I present in the order in which she did them. She saw that the purpose of all these techniques was to help her strengthen her conviction in her rational belief.

Rational-emotive imagery (REI)

I first suggested that Linda practise REI at least three times a day for 10 minutes per day. She agreed to do this and we decided together that she would do it before breakfast in her bedroom, after lunch in the quiet room at work and before supper in her bedroom. She foresaw no obstacles to her doing this. I gave her a set of written instructions on how to implement the technique (Dryden, 2001).

The attack-response technique

Having taught Linda how to use the attack-response technique, I suggested that she carry out the technique in writing before our next session. She agreed to do this on Saturday afternoon at 1 pm in her bedroom. Again, Linda foresaw no obstacles to her doing this. Again I gave her a set of written instructions on how to implement the technique (Dryden, 2001).

Acting on her rational beliefs while rehearsing these beliefs

After Linda had done the first two assignments she agreed to talk to her boss about him breaking his promise to promote her while rehearsing her rational belief. Before she did it we role-played the conversation with me playing her boss. Linda briefed me a little about her boss and then rehearsed her rational belief before the role-play. She was able to act on this rational belief during the role-play after which I gave her some feedback about how she could improve her assertion skills. Again she foresaw no obstacle to doing this in reality and she had already scheduled the meeting to see her boss.

Step 20: reviewing homework assignments

I reviewed each of the following assignments with Linda.

Rational-emotive imagery

Linda practised REI and reported no problems with it. I asked her to tell me how she used the technique and discovered that she used it correctly. She said that it helped her to 'feel her way' into the frame of mind of her rational belief at times when she reviewed her boss's broken promise in her mind.

The attack-response technique

Here I will present what Linda gave me and I will provide the same comment in italics that I gave her verbally in the session.

Rational belief: My boss is not bad for breaking his promise to promote me. He is fallible and does not have to keep his promise.

[Conviction rating of rational belief = 35%]

Attack: But bosses are supposed to keep their promises. He is my boss and therefore he absolutely should have kept his promise to me.

Response: That may hold true on the planet 'Fairness', but not on the planet 'Earth'. On Earth, people can and do sometimes break their promises. This is what happened with my boss on this occasion and sadly he acted according to what was in his mind at the time. He did not have to do what I wanted him to do. If he had to, he would have no choice but to keep his promise. But he did have a choice and unfortunately he made the wrong choice.

Attack: But that makes him a bad person.

Response: No it doesn't. It makes him fallible.

[Windy's observation: I suggested to Linda that it would

have been a good idea to expand on this point and stress what fallible means and how it applies to her boss's behaviour in this episode.]

Attack: But that's a cop-out.

Response: No, it's not. It's an explanation. I am not saying that he is not responsible for breaking his promise and I am not saying that his behaviour is not bad. His behaviour was bad and he is responsible for his behaviour, but this does not mean that he is a bad person. He is a human being with many different facets and can't be defined by breaking his promise to promote me.

[Conviction rating of original rational belief = 80%]

Linda found this exercise particularly helpful in strengthening her conviction in her rational belief. She pointed to the comparison she made between the planet 'Fairness' and the planet 'Earth' as being particularly persuasive and subsequently she reported that whenever she made herself unhealthily angry thinking about the broken promise, she reminded herself: 'This is Planet Earth, not Planet "Fairness". He does not have to be fair' and this helped her to feel constructively annoyed instead. This often happens when clients use the insights from RECBT. They put it into their own language and use their own imagery and when they do so, it is particularly persuasive to them.

Acting on her rational beliefs while rehearsing these beliefs

As agreed, Linda spoke to her boss about him breaking his promise to promote her. She rehearsed her rational belief beforehand and managed to think rationally about his broken promise throughout their conversation. Linda started out by checking the facts as she saw them: that he had told her that she was doing good work and that he was going to promote her and then when the time came he didn't. Her boss agreed with these facts. Linda then told him that she was annoyed that he broke his promise and wanted to understand why. Her boss said that he was prevented from promoting her by his superior who had put a block on all promotions for financial reasons. He admitted that he was wrong not to meet with her to tell her this, but did not do so because he was scared that she might be angry with him. They resolved to discuss the issue again at Linda's next appraisal.

Linda was very pleased with how she managed herself in the meeting. She considered the work we had done on her emotional problem (as outlined in this book) to be central to the positive outcome she experienced. After the meeting she experienced a sense of closure and as a result was ready to resume her coaching work with me on the personal objectives we had set at the outset.

Step 21: revisiting and questioning 'A' if necessary

Linda and I did not have to do any work here because it was clear that her adversity at 'A', namely 'My boss broke his promise to promote me' was true. Her boss even admitted this at their meeting.

Part 5

Epilogue

I hope you can see how the work I did with Linda on her emotional problem was consistent with the step-by-step guide that I discussed in Part 3 of this book. The work I did with Linda spanned three sessions with the bulk of the work being done in two sessions and our review of her meeting with her boss and the resultant decision to resume our work on her personal objectives taking place in the third session.

Before closing, I want to make a few general observations about the work that I did with Linda and about the step-by-step guide that I have discussed and illustrated in this book

How many sessions?

I am often asked the question concerning how many sessions should one devote to helping a coaching client deal with an emotional problem before resuming with more traditional coaching work. There is, actually, no simple answer to this question. As my good friend and colleague, Dr. Arnold Lazarus would say 'It depends' (Dryden, 1991). I would say that it depends on the following factors.

The complexity of the emotional problem

In general, the more complex a client's emotional problem, the more sessions you will need to devote to helping your client address it effectively.

The client's receptivity to RECBT

In general, the less receptive your client is to RECBT, the more sessions you will need to deal with your client's doubts, reservations and objections to the RECBT model. Of course, if it turns out that this model does not make sense to your client or that she cannot or does not want to use it to address her emotional problem, then you will need to refer her to someone who can help her to address this problem before returning to you for more traditional coaching work.

The skill level of the coach in using the RECBT model

In general, the less developed your RECBT skills, the more sessions you will need to devote to helping your client address her emotional problem. I have been using RECBT for over 30 years and without wanting to sound immodest, I have a high level of skill in using it to help clients address their emotional problems both within a coaching context and a counselling or psychotherapy context. Thus, you should not expect to deal with your clients' specific emotional problems within a coaching context as quickly as I did with Linda's emotional problem until you have developed your skills in using RECBT. How do you do this? Initially by attending courses in RECBT and then getting supervision on your work from an RECBT supervisor. I am happy to respond by email (windy@thedrydens.clara.net) to requests for relevant information on training and supervision.

Using the step-by-step model: a reminder

I want to reiterate a point that I made earlier in the book concerning the use of the step-by-step guide that I presented in Part 3 of the book and illustrated in Part 4. There are advantages and disadvantages of such a guide.

Advantages of the step-by-step guide

The main advantage of the step-by-step guide is that it provides those new to RECBT with a breakdown of the steps needed to practise RECBT well when dealing with your clients' emotional problems within a coaching context. If such a guide were not available, then you may very well struggle unduly when you come to practise RECBT. Indeed, it was in response to trainees' requests for such a guide for use in counselling and psychotherapy that I developed it in the first place (see Dryden, DiGiuseppe & Neenan, 2010) and which I have now adapted for use when dealing with clients' emotional problems within a coaching context.

Some may argue that it is too lengthy and that there

should be a guide with fewer steps for beginners. I have some sympathy with this view and, indeed, my counselling and coaching colleague, Michael Neenan and I have written such a guide for trainee counsellors (Neenan & Dryden, 2006).

The reason that I prefer the longer version presented in this book is that it is easy for trainees to miss steps that the shorter guide omits and that are important to take in the practice of RECBT with certain clients. Indeed, when I have used the shorter guide and have given feedback to a trainee that he or she has missed an important step that does not appear in the shorter guide, their response has been, not unreasonably, that the step should have been included in the guide. So, my preference is to include all the relevant steps, as I have done in this book, and to stress that you may not need to employ them all with all of your clients. I would rather be over-inclusive and include steps that you may not need to use on every occasion than be under-inclusive and omit steps that you may need to use on some occasions, but that you can't use because you don't know about them. This is a personal view and I recognize the validity of the argument, favoured by Michael Neenan (see Neenan & Dryden, 2006) that a shorter guide is less confusing for trainees.

Disadvantages of the step-by-step guide

The main disadvantage of a step-by-step guide such as the one presented in this book is that it may stunt creativity if you follow it slavishly. Thus, there are some people who value such a guide not because it outlines a model of practice, but because in their mind it tells them exactly what to do and they think that they need to follow the steps in the precise order in which they are presented in every case with every client. This is not how to use the guide.

While I appreciate that as a beginner to RECBT it is comfortable using a guide such as the one I outlined in Part 3 of this book, however, you should only use it in this way until you have developed some competence in applying RECBT. Then, it is important that you use the steps flexibly and begin to improvise. As I said earlier in the book, the steps are like chords and scales. You need to become proficient in their use before you improvise. Having said that creative coaching depends on the creative implementation of techniques and strategies that are tailored for use with individual clients rather than using a 'one size fits all' approach. This point applies whether you are working to help your client overcome the obstacle of her emotional problem or to work towards reaching her personal objectives.

So learn your scales, but then improvise! On that note, we have reached the end of the book.

References

Beck, A. T. (1976). *Cognitive therapy and the emotional disorders.* New York: International Universities Press.

Bordin, E. S. (1979). The generalizability of the psychoanalytic concept of the working alliance. *Psychotherapy: Theory, Research and Practice, 16(3),* 252–260.

Buckley, A., & Buckley, C. (2006). *A guide to coaching and mental health: The recognition and management of psychological issues.* Hove: Routledge.

Dryden, W. (1986). Language and meaning in RET. *Journal of Rational-Emotive Therapy, 4(2),* 131–142.

Dryden, W. (1991). *A dialogue with Arnold Lazarus: 'It depends'.* Milton Keynes: Open University Press.

Dryden, W. (2001). *Reason to change: A rational emotive behaviour therapy (REBT) workbook.* Hove: Brunner-Routledge.

Dryden, W. (2006). *Counselling in a nutshell.* London: Sage.

Dryden, W. (2009). *Understanding emotional problems: The REBT perspective.* Hove: Routledge.

Dryden, W., DiGiuseppe, R., & Neenan, M. (2010). *A primer on rational emotive behavior therapy.* 3rd edition. Champaign, IL: Research Press.

Ellis, A. (1979). Discomfort anxiety. A new cognitive behavioral construct. Part 1. *Rational Living, 14(2),* 3–8.

Ellis, A. (1980). Discomfort anxiety. A new cognitive behavioral construct. Part 2. *Rational Living, 15(1),* 25–30.

Ellis, A (2005). *The myth of self-esteem.* Amherst, NY: Prometheus.

Ellis, A., & Maultsby, M. C. (1974). *Techniques for using rational-emotive imagery*. New York: Institute for Rational Living.

Neenan, M., & Dryden, W. (2006). *Rational emotive behaviour therapy in a nutshell*. London: Sage.

Index